NEXT STEPS IN THE "SPECIAL RELATIONSHIP"— IMPACT OF A U.S.-U.K. FREE TRADE AGREEMENT

JOINT HEARING

BEFORE THE

SUBCOMMITTEE ON TERRORISM, NONPROLIFERATION, ANDTRADE

AND THE

SUBCOMMITTEE ON EUROPE, EURASIA, AND EMERGING THREATS

OF THE

COMMITTEE ON FOREIGN AFFAIRS

HOUSE OF REPRESENTATIVES

ONE HUNDRED FIFTEENTH CONGRESS

FIRST SESSION

FEBRUARY 1, 2017

Serial No. 115–1

Printed for the use of the Committee on Foreign Affairs

Available via the World Wide Web: http://www.foreignaffairs.house.gov/ or
http://www.gpo.gov/fdsys/

U.S. GOVERNMENT PUBLISHING OFFICE

23–885PDF   WASHINGTON : 2017

For sale by the Superintendent of Documents, U.S. Government Publishing Office
Internet: bookstore.gpo.gov   Phone: toll free (866) 512–1800; DC area (202) 512–1800
Fax: (202) 512–2104   Mail: Stop IDCC, Washington, DC 20402–0001

(II)

SUBCOMMITTEE ON TERRORISM, NONPROLIFERATION, AND TRADE

TED POE, Texas, *Chairman*

JOE WILSON, South Carolina
DARRELL E. ISSA, California
PAUL COOK, California
SCOTT PERRY, Pennsylvania
LEE M. ZELDIN, New York
BRIAN J. MAST, Florida
THOMAS A. GARRETT, JR., Virginia

WILLIAM R. KEATING, Massachusetts
LOIS FRANKEL, Florida
BRENDAN F. BOYLE, Pennsylvania
DINA TITUS, Nevada
NORMA J. TORRES, California
BRADLEY SCOTT SCHNEIDER, Illinois

————

SUBCOMMITTEE ON EUROPE, EURASIA, AND EMERGING THREATS

DANA ROHRABACHER, California, *Chairman*

JOE WILSON, South Carolina
TED POE, Texas
TOM MARINO, Pennsylvania
JEFF DUNCAN, South Carolina
F. JAMES SENSENBRENNER, JR.,
  Wisconsin
FRANCIS ROONEY, Florida
BRIAN K. FITZPATRICK, Pennsylvania

GREGORY W. MEEKS, New York
BRAD SHERMAN, California
ALBIO SIRES, New Jersey
WILLIAM R. KEATING, Massachusetts
DAVID N. CICILLINE, Rhode Island
ROBIN L. KELLY, Illinois

CONTENTS

NEXT STEPS IN THE "SPECIAL RELATIONSHIP"—IMPACT OF A U.S.–U.K. FREE TRADE AGREEMENT

WEDNESDAY, FEBRUARY 1, 2017

HOUSE OF REPRESENTATIVES,
SUBCOMMITTEE ON TERRORISM, NONPROLIFERATION, AND TRADE
AND
SUBCOMMITTEE ON EUROPE, EURASIA, AND EMERGING THREATS,
COMMITTEE ON FOREIGN AFFAIRS,
Washington, DC.

The subcommittees met, pursuant to notice, at 10:05 a.m., in room 2172, Rayburn House Office Building, Hon. Ted Poe (chairman of the Subcommittee on Terrorism, Nonproliferation, and Trade) presiding.

Mr. POE. The subcommittee will come to order. Without objection, all members may have 5 days to submit statements, questions, and extraneous materials for the record subject to the length limitation in the rules.

The Chair will recognize itself for an opening statement. I understand this is one of the first, if not the first, hearing since Congress has come back into session. And I think it is quite appropriate that we have this hearing dealing with the United States and the United Kingdom.

This past summer British citizens chose to reclaim their economic independence. In a landmark referendum, they decided to leave the European Union, take charge of their future, especially their economic future.

Now in the wake of Brexit, it is important that we preserve, as Winston Churchill once said in 1946, "the special relationship between the United States and the United Kingdom." The two nations are bound together by a shared history, a common language, well, maybe it is a common language, I am not sure being from Texas, but anyway, and a friendship that reaches back hundreds of years. I think the United States and the United Kingdom are an economic family separated by a bit of water.

For over 200 years our countries have partnered economically to preserve peace and security worldwide. Even from the trenches of World War I to the mountains of Afghanistan, men and women in both countries have spilled blood together on the battlefield. Our relationship is deep and it is special. A trade deal represents another opportunity to deepen that relationship to the benefit of both countries.

(1)

The previous administration threatened to put the United Kingdom at the back of the queue for a trade deal. But that kind of snub to our greatest ally is exactly the opposite of what we should be doing. A bilateral agreement will enhance the flow of commerce and boost the welfare of our economies. Trade deals that do not help the United States are going to be a thing of the past. A bilateral trade agreement can be beneficial to both of our interests.

The United Kingdom shares many values and business practices with the United States, and our similarities will help ensure a smooth negotiation process, as neither side will be forced into making hard concessions. For example, because Britain's workers are paid about the same rate as Americans, we do not have to worry about American manufacturers moving factories to the English countryside and jobs will not be sent overseas. We will be able to streamline regulations and reduce barriers to trade. And that means more consumers for U.S. goods.

Our two countries already enjoy close economic ties. No country receives more investment from Britain than the United States. And the United States is the largest investor in the United Kingdom. In my home State of Texas, the United Kingdom is the number one foreign direct investor. It sends over $2.5 billion a year to the Texas economy. And we like that. This investment has helped to bring more than 87,000 jobs to Texas. And Texas is a great place to do business. And the United Kingdom sees this.

These kinds of gains are not limited to Texas alone. Every day over 1 million Americans go to work for British companies based in the United States. It is critical we do not turn our backs on trade.

Houston is dependent on a free flow of trade. The Port of Houston is our economic hub. We are an export port. We make things, use as many as we can, and we sell the rest. About 50 percent of the Houston economy is based on the Port of Houston.

So trade is vital to our economy. But that does not mean that the United States has to give away the ranch to get a trade deal done. We can have free trade, and we can have fair trade. Fair trade for both countries. Free trade for both countries. We can level the playing field for American business, give American goods better access to consumers around the world, and increase jobs.

The new administration has expressed its preference for bilateral deals over more cumbersome and sometimes very political multilateral agreements. A bilateral deal with the United Kingdom is a great place to start. Once the U.K. is able to throw off the shackles, in my opinion, of the European Union's restrictive trade policies, there will be better opportunities for growth and investment.

A free trade deal between the United Kingdom and the United States will be an important symbol of our dedication of promoting economic freedom. Together we can come up with the gold standard for free trade deals. This deal could serve as a model for future deals or maybe even open up jobs in other nations.

This hearing gives us a time opportunity to examine what the U.S.-U.K. trade deal might look like, and discuss how to move forward. I look forward to hearing from our witnesses about how we can achieve that goal and take the next step in our special relationship.

I now recognize the ranking member on the TNT Subcommittee, Mr. Bill Keating from Massachusetts, for his opening statement.

Mr. KEATING. Thank you, Chairman Poe. And it is great to be joined by Chairman Rohrabacher and Ranking Member Meeks as well. This is a very timely and important foreign policy issue to address in our first hearing of the 115th Congress.

Thank you as well to our witnesses for being here and adding to the discussion with your expertise on the topic of trade and our partnership with Europe.

The United States indeed has a long and enduring special relationship with the United Kingdom. Our longstanding alliance has withstood numerous wars and conflicts, and in recent decades has been a critical force behind efforts to eradicate the threat of terrorism.

Our trade and investment relationship with the United Kingdom is substantial, and both our countries benefit greatly from these close economic ties.

This relationship encountered a new diplomatic landscape last summer when the people of Britain voted in a referendum to leave the European Union. This outcome was surprising to many, including myself. And as a close partner to both the U.K. and the EU, we in Congress are keenly interested in the process by which Britain exits the EU, and how the United States may continue to pursue a coherent foreign policy with these important partners. It is therefore also necessary to be careful that the politics on both sides of the Atlantic around Brexit and how it will unfold do not undermine the significance of the U.S. relationship with the EU nor of its relationship with Britain.

U.S. ties with the EU in trade, and defense, intelligence, and across a broad range of issues has strengthened our economy and helped make us more secure. As a co-chair of TTIP caucus, I welcome the trade negotiation between the U.S. and the EU, with our economies representing nearly half the global GDP. And with the U.S. and the EU being each other's largest overall trade and investment partner, this agreement would support jobs, remove trade barriers, and improve market access for our goods and services.

It would also allow the U.S. and the EU to contribute to setting high standards for global trade; standards that reflect fair treatment of workers, environmental concerns, safeguarding intellectual property and fair trade.

In the challenges we face, both economic and in terms of security, the strategic importance of our relationship with the EU is undeniable. Other impacts of Brexit such as the effects on the longstanding efforts of the U.S. to help broker Irish peace and reduce division there are also of great concern.

I have become concerned by suggestions that maintaining our special relationship with Britain would come at the expense of promoting robust transatlantic relations with the rest of Europe. These relationships are not mutually exclusive. The U.S. benefits in critical ways from each of them. Prime Minister May recently spoke to this point, emphasizing that a strong EU is positive and critical for security. And I believe that security includes strong economic relations.

So I am pleased that both the European and Trade Subcommittees are holding this hearing today to address U.S.-U.K. relations and the impact of a U.S.-U.K. free trade agreement, because the question is not a question to be considered in a vacuum. U.S.-U.K. ties are unique but they need not be exclusive. To reinforce a sentiment of Prime Minister May, this is not a time to turn inward.

I yield back.

Mr. POE. I thank the gentleman. The Chair recognizes the subcommittee chairman, Mr. Dana Rohrabacher, for his opening statement.

Mr. ROHRABACHER. Thank you very much, Your Honor. And good morning. I would like to welcome all the new and returning members of the Europe, Eurasian Subcommittee. And I am looking forward to a very productive Congress.

This is our first hearing, the joint hearing with Judge Poe's subcommittee as well. I am happy to be working this session again with Ranking Member Gregory Meeks. And we have had an exemplary, positive and very, very fruitful relationship. And again I would like to thank Chairman Poe for initiating this hearing.

In the lead-up to last year's Brexit vote, there was an onslaught of hyperbolic language. It was almost like the language that we saw in our own last election as to what would happen if there wasn't the outcome that certain people in the press wanted to happen. But that language that we heard about Brexit regarded many forms of disaster that would result from Britain leaving the EU.

Some naysayers even predicted that if England were to leave the EU, the confusion of the exiting, and then the confusion to the existing order might be of such a magnitude that America would be so confused that we would elect an out-of-control President. Okay. It is a joke.

Mr. POE. We got it.

Mr. ROHRABACHER. You got it. Okay. Well, last June the voters in the U.K. made their wishes known. And Prime Minister May is acting accordingly.

From the perspective of the United States, our interests are served when the United Kingdom is strong and has a close functioning relationship with the United States, with us.

The EU was founded on a vision of a Europe, democratic, united in principle, efficiently and fairly coordinated by a supranational Parliament and a multinational bureaucracy. Well, clearly the British people don't think the EU reality is what the original visionaries had in mind. The American presence did not see the original vision, however, as a slight to the United States. Even though we weren't invited.

President Eisenhower welcomed the beginning of an integrated Europe, and Presidents like President Reagan, who I think I remember him saying a few words about this, supported what he called the European community, hoping that someday the Central European countries newly freed from Soviet occupation, which of course was our goal, would provide an opportunity for stability, progress, and freedom on the entire European continent.

Our discussion today is not about the United States picking sides but about working with our most reliable Atlantic partner and how recent decisions affect the long-term trends there. Perhaps we should be looking at, as Judge Poe just mentioned, a new bilateral free trade agreement between the United States and the U.K. which could be a model for other countries as well.

While I have yet to fully examine many of the specifics about such a deal, I am interested in hearing about that today, I think it makes sense to tie down a treaty that is mutually beneficial, that is a good deal for the British and a good deal for us.

And with that said, I am looking forward to this hearing. Thank you, Judge Poe, for calling this hearing. And I am looking forward to hearing from the witnesses.

Mr. POE. The gentleman yields back. And the Chair will recognize the ranking member—started to make a doctor out of you— Mr. Gregory Meeks for his opening statement.

Mr. MEEKS. Thank you, Chairman Poe. And I likewise want to also thank Chairman Rohrabacher. We have formed a good team of free and open and good debate on the European Subcommittee. And I look forward to another exciting 115th Congress and continuing bilateral dialogue to further American interests abroad regardless of whose party is in power.

I also want to thank Ranking Member Keating, along with Chairman Poe, for having this combined hearing today. And today's hearing is an important one, and the first in the House to address the Brexit vote and its consequences for transatlantic relations. The decision by the EU, combined with President Trump's victory here, has set the stage, in my opinion, for uncertainty.

Even today's hearing is very theoretical and based on a future successful Brexit negotiation with the EU, whatever form that may take, because we don't know what form it will take. So it can only be theoretical today. Only then will we be able to discuss specific bilateral trade policy with the U.K.

Now, I do think a strong relationship between the United States and the U.K. is certainly in both parties' interests and good for the world. This is first and foremost based on defense cooperation, intel sharing, and by extension, NATO.

In the trade world, Prime Minister May says she wants the U.K. to be a champion of global trade. President Trump, depending on the day, is a protectionist interfering in business decisions at home, and threatened to tear apart trade deals internationally. Trade negotiations are complicated. And when negotiating with the U.K., I am certain we will run into roadblocks, for example, on health services and agriculture.

Our cultural ties will only stretch so far when it comes to business, just as we have done a lot of work already dealing with TTIP. Furthermore, the Republican administration and Prime Minister May have vastly different views on the future of the EU and Russia.

Whereas Mrs. May was clear in her support of a strong EU when she told the Republicans in Philadelphia, "We are not turning our backs on the EU or in the interests and values we share. It remains overwhelmingly in our interest," she said, "and those of the wider world that the EU should succeed."

On the other hand, Mr. Trump has expressed harsh skepticism of the EU and NATO, symbols of our shared values. On Russia, Mrs. May's government has been a leader in uniting the EU in sanctions on Russia for its war in Ukraine. And has continuously encouraged support for a strong NATO presence on its eastern borders.

As we all know, these views are not shared completely by our current administration. And this confusion will be tested by the Kremlin. Any olive branch to Moscow is naive and, frankly, I think dangerous without first assuring our friends and allies in the U.K. who share our ideals and commitment to freedom.

In conclusion, I view the future of our special relationship as one that is based on mutual security, common ideals and values, and, finally, on economics and trade.

Looking at a future post-Brexit trade deal with all of its variables is a difficult task. It may be easy to get a sound bite out of support from our President who may not know the Lipscomb Treaty, but it would be much more difficult between negotiators acting solely on their national interests.

As a supporter of TTIP negotiations, I remain optimistic of the future of transatlantic trade and urge stronger transatlantic ties. The European project, after all, is a peace project firmly aligned with American interests and designed to protect our liberal democratic ideas. And I look forward to hearing from our witnesses about how a new U.K.-U.S. trade deal can help us in that goal. And I yield back.

Mr. POE. The gentleman yields back his time. The Chair will recognize any other members for 1 minute if they wish to make an opening statement. And the Chair will put all members on notice that the 1 minute will be 1 minute.

Okay. The Chair recognizes the gentleman from California, Mr. Sherman, for his statement.

Mr. SHERMAN. Been here 20 years. Never seen the body politic so strained, frayed. Chairman Royce has said this is the most bipartisan committee in Congress. I hope it is true.

We have got to avoid the temptation to evaluate everything, even a British trade deal, through the prison of whether it is a vehicle to express our support or opposition to President Trump. I know Nigel Farage campaigned with Trump. But that is not a reason for Democrats to reject, the Republicans to support any particular trade deal. A million of the British people have signed a petition to exclude Donald Trump from their territory. That is not a reason for Democrats to support, or Republicans to reject a trade deal. We have got—if we want just a symbol, then we don't have to look at the trade deal except its cover.

I suggest instead we not judge it by its cover but by the contents that have yet to be written and ask what is in it for American working families.I look forward to talking to our witnesses about what should be in it and evaluating it in the sense of jobs, not a job evaluation for the administration.

Mr. POE. The gentleman yields back his time. The Chair recognizes the gentleman from Rhode Island, Mr. Cicilline, for a 1-minute statement.

Mr. CICILLINE. Thank you, Mr. Chairman. I want to thank Chairman Rohrabacher and Ranking Member Meeks for holding this joint hearing. And would also like to say, as a new member of this subcommittee, I look forward to working with both of you.

The United Kingdom is one of our oldest and most important allies. And it has always been a reliable friend in our times of greatest need. In Iraq and Afghanistan, more than 600 British troops were killed during fighting alongside American troops.

The United Kingdom continues to be a key partner in combatting global terrorism. In addition, the United Kingdom is a vital trading partner. The U.S. exports more than $51 billion in goods to the U.K. annually, including approximately $50 million from my home State of Rhode Island in 2015.

In June of last year, the United Kingdom became the first country to plan to withdraw from the European Union. This decision will have wide-ranging effects on international markets and U.S. security relationships in the U.K. and in Europe.

I welcome the witnesses and look forward to hearing from you today about what these effects will be and how they will shape the special relationship between the United States and the United Kingdom in the years to come.

And with that I yield back.

Mr. POE. I thank the gentleman from Rhode Island. Are there any other members that wish to make an opening statement?

The Chair will now introduce the three witnesses that we have. First of all, without objection, all the witnesses' prepared statements will be made part of the record. I ask that each witness please keep your presentation to no more than 5 minutes. After 5 minutes you may hear the sound of a gavel. That means stop. But we do have your statements, and they are part of the record.

Mr. Nile Gardiner is director of the Heritage Foundation's Margaret Thatcher Center for Freedom. Prior to joining Heritage in 2002, he was a foreign policy researcher for former British Prime Minister Margaret Thatcher.

Mr. Simon Lester is a trade policy analyst with Cato's Herbert Stiefel Center for Trade Policies. His research focuses on WTO disputes, regional trade agreements, protectionism, and the history of international trade law.

Dr. Daniel Hamilton is founding director of the Center for Transatlantic Relations at Johns Hopkins University School of Advanced and International Studies. He has held a variety of senior positions at the United States Department of State, including deputy assistant secretary for European Affairs.

Dr. Gardiner, we will start with you. You have 5 minutes.

STATEMENT OF NILE GARDINER, PH.D., DIRECTOR, MARGARET THATCHER CENTER FOR FREEDOM, THE HERITAGE FOUNDATION

Mr. GARDINER. Good morning. Thank you very much. Chairman Poe, Chairman Rohrabacher, and distinguished members, thank you for the opportunity to testify before both of your committees today. For reasons of time, with your permission, I will be summarizing parts of my written statement.

It is fitting that today's hearing is taking place just days after the inauguration of a new U.S. President, and just months after a new British Prime Minister entered Downing Street. President Donald Trump and Prime Minister Theresa May met last Friday in Washington, and declared their intention to advance a U.S.-U.K.

free trade agreement. The Trump presidency is in a strong position to revitalize the special relationship by working together with Congress and the Government of the United Kingdom.

The Anglo-American alliance is a vital partnership that rests upon deep-seated cooperation in defense, trade, intelligence, and a host of other areas stretching from educational exchange to the arts. Britain's decision to leave the European Union should be viewed as a hugely positive development by Congress because it offers tremendous opportunities for Britain and the United States to strengthen that partnership.

The Trump administration should make a U.S.-U.K. free trade deal a foreign policy priority. There is already strong support from Capitol Hill for a free trade agreement, between the United States and the United Kingdom, with at least five pieces of Congressional legislation urging such a deal. Such an agreement between the world's largest and fifth largest economies would significantly advance prosperity on both sides of the Atlantic. It would be a force generator for economic liberty through genuine bilateral free trade based upon the principles of sovereignty and economic freedom.

A free trade agreement would boost both Britain's and America's economies while also strengthening the Anglo-American special relationship, for decades the engine and beating heart of the free world. It would also act as a model for other free trade agreements that Britain will likely sign with countries across the globe from Australia and Canada to India and Singapore.

A stronger Britain on the world stage, able to act as a truly sovereign independent nation, is a far better partner for the United States. Outside of an inward-looking, declining European Union, Great Britain is uniquely placed to rebuild its military might, revitalize the NATO alliance together with the Americans, and stand up to the enemies of the free world.

America has a deep interest in helping Brexit to succeed and in Britain flourishing outside the EU. Britain must help America to lead the free world with strength, resolve, and conviction. The special relationship is a great force for good in the world. And its return should be welcomed by all who cherish the spirit of freedom and liberty.

President Trump should instruct the U.S. trade representative and the White House National Trade Council to fast track the pursuit of a U.S.-U.K. trade pact by putting forward clear negotiating objectives pursuant to congressional guidance that will advance the special relationship. The free trade deal should be implemented within 90 days after Britain leaves the European Union, which is expected to be by the end of March 2019. The overriding goal should be to sign the best deal possible by then.

Under a free trade agreement, the U.S. and U.K. must make it easier for Americans and Britons engaged in lawful finance and commerce to work together. The deal should aim for the elimination of all tariff barriers between the U.S. and the U.K., two nations with highly developed economies, skilled workforces, and comparable wage levels. Such a deal would create jobs on both sides of the Atlantic and enhance investment opportunities.

Talks between Washington and London on a U.S.-U.K. free trade deal can begin immediately. The United Kingdom has the full right to begin discussions on trade agreements with countries outside of the European Union before it formally exits the EU. As the Lawyers for Britain Group has pointed out, it is false to claim, as some European commission officials have done, that Britain cannot engage in such discussions as an EU member.

I urge President Trump to work closely with Congress. This must be a joint initiative by the White House and the House of Representatives and Senate. A U.S.-U.K. free trade agreement would advance prosperity on both sides of the Atlantic, and will be a historic move forward that will benefit future generations of both Americans and Britons.

The free trade pact should be a catalyst for advancing freedom to trade and for promoting economic freedom in both countries. It would be a powerful statement reflecting a shared commitment to a free and open investment environment between the two nations. This is a bilateral trade deal, not a multilateral one, which makes negotiations far simpler than they might otherwise be. In contrast to the hugely flawed proposed Transatlantic Trade and Investment Partnership, TTIP, between the U.S. and EU, this is not about importing regulations and expanding big government. It is about empowering individuals and freeing trade. We do not need hundreds of pages of fine print to move forward with such a deal. It should be streamlined and readily understandable to anyone who wishes to read it.

In conclusion, a U.S.-U.K. FTA would be an outstanding example of a special relationship in practice, further bringing together two nations with a shared history, culture, and language, as well as a deep commitment to liberty. It should also act as a role model for future free trade agreements between the United States and other key allies across the world.

Britain's exit from the European Union will make the partnership between Great Britain and the United States even stronger. And a free trade agreement will be at the very heart of that alliance. Today, in large part due to the robust support of Members of Congress, Britain stands at the front of the queue for a trade deal with the United States and not at the back.

Thank you for giving me the opportunity to testify before you today. Britain's impending exit from the European Union has opened a new world of opportunity for the United Kingdom. Opportunities that should also be embraced by the United States and all who believe in liberty, sovereignty, and self-determination. Thank you.

[The prepared statement of Mr. Gardiner follows:]

CONGRESSIONAL TESTIMONY

Next Steps in the "Special Relationship":
Impact of a U.S.-U.K. Free Trade Agreement

Testimony of Dr. Nile Gardiner
Director, Margaret Thatcher Center for Freedom
The Heritage Foundation

Testimony before
House Committee on Foreign Affairs Joint Subcommittee Hearing:
Subcommittee on Terrorism, Nonproliferation, and Trade; Subcommittee on
Europe, Eurasia, and Emerging Threats

February 1, 2017

Chairman Poe, Chairman Rohrabacher, and distinguished Members: Thank you for the opportunity to testify before both of your committees.

It is fitting that today's hearing is taking place just days after the inauguration of a new U.S. President and just months after a new British Prime Minister entered Downing Street. President Donald Trump and Prime Minister Theresa May met last Friday in Washington and declared their intention to advance a U.S.–U.K. free trade agreement. The Trump presidency is in a strong position to revitalize the Special Relationship by working together with Congress and the government of the United Kingdom.

The Anglo–American alliance is a vital partnership that rests upon deep-seated cooperation in defense, trade, intelligence, and a host of other areas stretching from educational exchange to the arts. **Britain's decision to leave the European Union should** be viewed as a hugely positive development by Congress because it offers tremendous opportunities for Britain and the United States to strengthen that partnership.

The Trump Administration should make a U.S.–U.K. free trade deal a foreign policy priority. There is already strong support on Capitol Hill for a free trade agreement between the United States and the United Kingdom with at least five pieces of **Congressional legislation urging such a deal. Such an agreement between the world's** largest and fifth-largest economies would significantly advance prosperity on both sides of the Atlantic. It would be a force generator for economic liberty through genuine bilateral free trade based upon the principles of sovereignty and economic freedom.

America has a vital economic stake in the United Kingdom. As the Congressional Research Service notes, **Britain is America's largest services trading partner**, and the $5 trillion of U.S. corporate assets in the U.K. represents 22 percent of total U.S. corporate overseas assets.[1] **Britain is America's** largest foreign direct investor, and roughly a million U.S. jobs depend on British companies based in America. British foreign direct investment (FDI) in the United States in 2015 amounted to over $483 billion.[2] More than 1.25 million people are employed by U.S. affiliates in the U.K., and U.S. FDI in the U.K. was approximately $593 billion in 2015.[3]

---

[1] Derek E. Mix, "The United Kingdom: Background and Relations with the United States," Congressional Research Service *Report for Members and Committees of Congress*, April 29, 2015, https://fas.org/sgp/crs/row/RL33105.pdf.

[2] Rudy Telles, Jr., "Foreign Direct Investment in the United States: Update to 2013 Report," U.S. Department of Commerce, Economics and Statistics Administration. Office of the Chief Economist, *ESA Issue Brief* No. 02-16, June 20, 2016, http://www.esa.doc.gov/sites/default/files/foreign-direct-investment-in-the-united-states-update-2016.pdf.

[3] James K. Jackson, Shayerah Ilias Akhtar, and Derek E. Mix, "Economic Implications of a United Kingdom Exit from the European Union," Congressional Research Service *Report for Members and Committees of Congress*, July 14, 2016, https://fas.org/sgp/crs/row/R44559.pdf.

Strengthening the Special Relationship by Advancing Freedom to Trade with the United Kingdom

A free trade agreement would boost both Britain's and America's economies while also strengthening the Anglo–American Special Relationship, for decades the engine and beating heart of the free world. It would also act as a model for other free trade agreements that Britain will likely sign with countries across the globe, from Australia and Canada to India and Singapore. Free trade has been the essence of Britain's success as a global power for centuries. The EU, with its protectionist mindset and outright hostility to economic freedom, has constrained Britain's ability to trade freely for over four decades and has held back Britain's economic potential.

A stronger Britain on the world stage, able to act as a truly sovereign, independent nation, is a far better partner for the United States. Outside of an inward-looking, declining EU, Great Britain is uniquely placed to rebuild its military might, revitalize the NATO alliance together with the Americans, and stand up to the enemies of the free world, from Russia to Iran and ISIS.

America has a deep interest in helping Brexit to succeed and in Britain's flourishing outside the EU. Britain must help America to lead the free world with strength, resolve, and conviction. The Special Relationship is a great force for good in the world, and its return should be welcomed by all who cherish the spirit of freedom and liberty.

As Margaret Thatcher observed in a speech to the Foreign Relations Council of Chicago, "the special relationship does exist, it does count and it must continue, because the United States needs friends in the lonely task of world leadership."[4]

Recommendations for Congress and the Executive Branch

President Trump should instruct the U.S. Trade Representative and the White House National Trade Council to fast-track the pursuit of a U.S.–U.K. trade pact by putting forward clear negotiating objectives, pursuant to congressional guidance, that will advance the Special Relationship between the two countries. The free trade deal should be implemented within 90 days after Britain leaves the EU, which is expected to be by the end of March 2019. The overriding goal should be to sign the best deal possible by then.

Under a free trade agreement, the U.S. and U.K. must make it easier for Americans and Britons engaged in lawful finance and commerce to work together. The deal should aim for the elimination of all tariff barriers between the United States and the United Kingdom, two nations with highly developed economies, skilled workforces, and comparable wage levels. Such a deal would create jobs on both sides of the Atlantic and enhance investment opportunities.

---

[4]Margaret Thatcher, "Speech to Foreign Relations Council of Chicago," June 17, 1991, http://www.margaretthatcher.org/document/108275.

Talks between Washington and London on a U.S.–U.K. free trade deal can begin immediately. The United Kingdom has the full right to begin discussions on trade agreements with countries outside of the European Union before it formally exits the EU. As the Lawyers for Britain group has pointed out, it is false to claim, as some European Commission officials have done, that Britain cannot engage in such discussions as an EU member: **"This view has no support from the EU Treaties or the Court of Justice of the** European Union (CJEU): the EU may not prevent the UK negotiating and entering into such treaties providing that they will not come into force until the UK withdraws from the EU."[5]

I urge President Trump to work closely with Congress. This must be a joint initiative by the White House and the House of Representatives and Senate. A U.S.–U.K. free trade agreement will advance prosperity on both sides of the Atlantic and will be a historic move forward that will benefit future generations of both Americans and Britons. The free trade pact should be a catalyst for advancing freedom to trade and for promoting economic freedom in both countries. It would be a powerful statement reflecting a shared commitment to a free and open investment environment between the two countries.

This is a bilateral trade deal, not a multilateral one, which makes negotiations far simpler than they might otherwise be. In contrast to the hugely flawed proposed Transatlantic Trade and Investment Partnership (TTIP) between the U.S. and the EU, this is not about importing regulations and expanding big government. It is about empowering individuals and freeing trade. We do not need hundreds of pages of fine print to move forward with such a deal. It should be streamlined and readily understandable to anyone who wishes to read it.

In conclusion, a U.S.–U.K. FTA would be an outstanding example of the Anglo–American Special Relationship in practice, further bringing together two great nations with a shared history, culture, and language as well as a deep commitment to liberty. As my colleague Dr. Ted Bromund and I have argued in a Heritage Foundation paper, "a U.S.–U.K. free trade area should serve as a symbol of and a real contribution toward a shared Anglo–American rejection of supranational control and the shared belief that government must be based on sovereignty and freedom."[6] It should also act as a role model for future free trade agreements between the United States and other key allies across the world.

Britain's exit from the European Union will make the partnership between Great Britain and the United States even stronger, and a free trade agreement will be at the very heart of that alliance. Today, in large part due to the robust support of Members of Congress, Britain stands at the front of the queue for a trade deal with the United States and not at

---

[5]Francis Hoar, "Negotiating International Trade Treaties Before Exit," Lawyers for Britain, http://www.lawyersforbritain.org/int-trade-before-exit.shtml.

[6]Ted R. Bromund and Nile Gardiner, "Freedom from the EU: Why Britain and the U.S. Should Pursue a U.S.–U.K. Free Trade Area," Heritage Foundation *Backgrounder* No. 2951, September 26, 2014. http://www.heritage.org/research/reports/2014/09/freedom-from-the-eu-why-britain-and-the-us-should-pursue-a-usuk-free-trade-area.

the back. Theresa May put it well in her speech to Congressional leaders in Philadelphia **last week when she declared that** "[s]uch an agreement would see us taking that next step in the Special Relationship that exists between us. Cementing and affirming one of the greatest forces for progress this world has ever known.... [L]et us renew the relationship that can lead the world towards the promise of freedom and prosperity....."[7]

Thank you for giving me the opportunity to testify before you today. Britain's impending exit from the European Union has opened a new world of opportunity for the United Kingdom, opportunities that should also be embraced by the United States and all who believe in liberty, sovereignty, and self-determination.

---

[7] The Rt. Hon. Theresa May, "Prime Minister's Speech to the Republican Party Conference 2017," Philadelphia, Pennsylvania, January 26, 2017, https://www.gov.uk/government/speeches/prime-ministers-speech-to-the-republican-party-conference-2017.

Mr. POE. Mr. Lester, 5 minutes.

STATEMENT OF MR. SIMON LESTER, TRADE POLICY ANALYST, HERBERT A. STIEFEL CENTER FOR TRADE POLICY STUDIES, CATO INSTITUTE

Mr. LESTER. Good morning. Chairman Poe, Ranking Member Keating, Chairman Rohrabacher, Ranking Member Meeks, and members of both subcommittees, thank you very much for the opportunity to come here today and speak on this important topic. I will be giving a summary of my written statement.

With the sometimes harsh rhetoric on trade during the recent Presidential campaign, and continuing over the past couple months, I and other free traders have been worried about the direction of U.S. trade policy. However, the positive talk from both Congress and the incoming administration about a U.S.-U.K. trade agreement has offered us some hope.

Trade negotiations have been struggling in recent years with more failures than successes. Perhaps a U.S.-U.K. agreement is just what we need to regain some momentum for trade liberalization. At the same time, we need to be realistic about its chances. Despite much early enthusiasm for an agreement, there will be significant hurdles on both sides of the Atlantic.

Turning first to the U.S. side, some advisers to the President Trump administration have talked about the possibility of a quick trade agreement with the U.K. However, just getting started will take some time. The United States has a model for trade agreements that has been fairly consistent for a decade now, with slight tweaks depending on which party holds power. However, given its criticism of U.S. trade policy during the campaign, the Trump administration is likely to re-evaluate this model. And its revision may take a little while to complete. Competing views within the administration will need to be reconciled, and stakeholders will need to be consulted. I am confident that the new administration will reach a decision on what it wants to see in a trade agreement. But this process could take a few months if not more.

But it is the U.K.'s side where the real challenges lie. The reason we can even have this discussion is because the U.K. is leaving the EU. But keep in mind, all that has happened so far is a referendum in which the British people voted to leave the EU. The formal withdrawal process has not even started yet. When the withdrawal process does begin, the U.K.'s limited government resources in this area will be strained, as it has relied on the European Commission to negotiate trade deals for decades now. This could slow down its efforts to negotiate new trade agreements.

In addition, there are political and legal hurdles to the U.K. negotiating an agreement with the U.S. right away. Some argue that there are legal limits on the extent to which the U.K. may negotiate its own trade agreements while it is still a member of the EU. In my view, the U.K. actually has a fair amount of leeway on this. But U.S. proponents of a U.S.-U.K. trade agreement should be aware of the issue. Even if it does not act as a legal bar to U.S.-U.K. talks, it could be a political hurdle. The U.K. needs to establish a new economic relationship with the EU, its most important trading partner, and thus will have to take into account the views of the Europeans on this.

Despite these hurdles, the size of the U.S. and U.K. economies and their significant trading relationship means that there would be great benefits from liberalizing trade between them. And that it is worth pursuing a deal.

In terms of the specific content of a U.S.-U.K. trade agreement, the two countries are at similar development levels and have many shared values. That should make negotiations easier. There will not be the sensitivities that arise for trade with certain developing countries. And some of the more controversial trade agreement provisions may, therefore, not be necessary. In this regard, labor protections and special dispute procedures for foreign investors could be excluded, and this could speed up the negotiating process.

The more issues that are included in the trade agreement, the longer it will take to complete the negotiations, and the more controversial the agreement will be. With these considerations in mind, the focus of a U.S.-U.K. trade agreement should be on eliminating tariffs, as many as politically possible, as well as adopting mutual recognition of standards and regulations so as to facilitate trade, in particular products and services. With the issues relating to domestic regulations, however, our ambitions should be modest. There is no need to deal with all products and services at once, which would take a long time and would delay completion of the agreement. Instead, it makes sense to select a few sectors, such as automobiles, pharmaceutical drugs, financial services, to address now, and then have a framework agreement under which the governments could deal with other sectors later.

Overall, in my view, prospects for a timely and economically significant U.S.-U.K. trade deal that focuses on these core trade issues are good. The successful negotiation here would be the first positive step forward for trade liberalization in quite some time, and could generate momentum for liberalization more broadly.

Thank you for your time, and I look forward to answering your questions.

[The prepared statement of Mr. Lester follows:]

Written Statement of Simon Lester,
Trade Policy Analyst, Herbert A. Stiefel Center for Trade Policy Studies, Cato Institute

before the

United States House of Representatives Subcommittees on Terrorism, Nonproliferation, and Trade, and Europe, Eurasia, and Emerging Threats

Next Steps in the "Special Relationship" – Impact of a US-UK Free Trade Agreement

February 1, 2017

Chairman Poe, Ranking Member Keating, Chairman Rohrabacher, Ranking Member Meeks, and members of both sub-committees, thank you very much for the opportunity to come here today and speak on this important topic.

With the sometimes harsh rhetoric on trade during the recent presidential campaign, and continuing over the past couple months, I and other free traders have been worried about the direction of US trade policy.

However, the positive talk from both Congress and the incoming administration about a US – UK trade agreement has offered us some hope. Trade negotiations have been struggling in recent years, with more failures than successes. Perhaps a US - UK agreement is just what we need to regain some momentum for trade liberalization.

At the same time, we need to be realistic about its chances. Despite much early enthusiasm for an agreement, there will be significant hurdles, on both sides of the Atlantic.

Turning first to the US side, some advisers to the Trump administration have talked about the possibility of a quick trade agreement with the UK. However, just getting started will take some time.

The United States has a model for trade agreements that has been fairly consistent for a decade now, with slight tweaks depending on which party holds the presidency. However, given its criticism of US trade policy during the campaign, the Trump administration is likely to reevaluate this model, and its revision may take a little while to complete. Competing views within the administration will need to be reconciled, and stakeholders will need to be consulted. I am confident that the new administration will eventually reach a decision on what it wants to see in a trade agreement, but this process could take a few months, if not more.

But it is the UK side where the real challenges lie. The reason we can even have this discussion is because the UK is leaving the EU. But keep in mind, all that has happened so far is a referendum, in which the British people voted to leave the EU. The formal withdrawal process has not even started yet. (The UK Supreme Court recently ruled that the UK government cannot legally trigger withdrawal until there is an act of Parliament authorizing it, which should happen soon.)

When the withdrawal process does begin, the UK's limited resources in this area will be strained, as it has relied on the European Commission to negotiate trade deals for decades now. The UK will have to hire hundreds of trade experts and set up trade institutions from scratch, as well as decide on its own framework for trade agreements. This could slow down its efforts to negotiate new trade agreements.

In addition, there are political and legal hurdles to the UK negotiating an agreement with the US right away. Some argue that there are limits on the extent to which the UK may negotiate its own trade agreements while it is still a member of the EU. In my view, the UK actually has a fair amount of leeway on this, but US proponents of a US - UK agreement should be aware of the issue. Even if it does not act as a legal bar to US - UK talks, it could be a political hurdle. The UK needs to establish a new economic relationship with the EU (its most important trading partner), and thus will have to take into account the views of the European leadership.

In addition, the precise nature of the relationship that the UK has with the EU will affect other countries' trade and investment with the UK. As a result, they may want to see the terms of the UK - EU deal before concluding their own. For example, what is the precise nature of the access producers in the UK have to the EU market? US companies selling intermediate goods to the UK will be affected if the finished goods have limited access to the EU. And how will UK regulations differ from the EU regulations that previously applied to the UK market? Conflicting standards between the UK and EU will have an impact on companies selling products to those markets.

Despite these hurdles, a US - UK trade agreement is worth pursuing. After the EU, the US is the UK's largest trading partner, and the UK is the 7th largest trading partner of the US. And in terms of the magnitude of the economies, the US is the largest in the world and the UK is number five. The size of the economies combined with the significant trading relationship between the two means that this deal would have substantial benefits for both economies, as increased competition leads to more choices and lower prices for consumers.

In terms of the specific content of a US - UK trade agreement, the two countries are at similar development levels, and have many shared values. That should make negotiations easier. There will not be the sensitivities that arise in relation to trade with certain developing countries, and some of the more controversial trade agreement provisions may therefore not be necessary. In this regard, labor protections and special dispute procedures for foreign investors could be excluded, which could speed up the process. It would be disappointing to have the US - UK trade negotiations turn into a 3 to 5-year slog, bogged down by disagreements over governance rules, as we have seen with other trade negotiations.

Written statement of Simon Lester, Cato Institute

More generally, a US - UK trade negotiation provides an opportunity to think carefully about the current model for US trade agreements. The Trans Pacific Partnership, the most recently completed US trade negotiation, has provisions on all of the following issues: Sanitary and Phytosanitary Measures; Technical Barriers to Trade; Investment; Electronic Commerce; Competition Policy; State-Owned Enterprises; Intellectual Property; Labor; Environment; Regulatory Coherence; and Transparency and Anti-Corruption. There were interest groups supporting the inclusion of each issue, and there may be good reasons to include some of them in trade agreements. At the same time, however, each new issue adds controversy and complexity to the trade negotiation process. The struggle to negotiate and ratify US trade agreements in recent years is attributable in part to their growing scope.

In this regard, it should be noted that the World Trade Organization contains fairly detailed rules on some of these issues, such as Sanitary and Phytosanitary Measures and Technical Barriers to Trade. Those rules have been applied successfully in resolving many trade disputes, and therefore replicating what is already available at the WTO in a bilateral and regional trade agreement may not be worth the effort.

With these considerations in mind, a US - UK trade agreement should focus on the following. First, while tariffs have been lowered over the years, some of them are still fairly high. The US and UK should aim to eliminate as many tariffs as politically possible, in as short a time-frame as possible. The ultimate goal should be zero tariffs on all trade between the US and UK. There will be interest groups who resist this, but the average person is better off with the increased competition and lower prices that result.

Second, discussions of recent trade negotiations often note that eliminating regulatory trade barriers will offer the most benefits. On this issue, as noted, some regulatory trade barriers are already prohibited through WTO obligations (for example, using domestic taxes and regulations to protect domestic industry from foreign competition is not allowed). Where FTAs could go further than the WTO is with mutual recognition of standards and regulations, so as to facilitate trade in particular products and services. In many products and services, UK standards and regulations are just as effective as US ones, and there would be great benefit in allowing goods and services that may be sold in one country to be sold in the other as well, without additional testing or certification.

Where domestic regulations are at issue, however, our ambitions should be modest (the high expectations on these issues for the US - EU trade talks may have slowed that negotiation down). Complete harmonization of the regulatory process and of substantive regulations is unlikely in a US - UK FTA. And there is no need to deal with all products and services at once, as it would take a long time to work out the details, cause a great deal of controversy, and likely delay completion of the agreement. Instead, it makes more sense to select a few sectors -- such as automobiles, pharmaceutical drugs, or financial services -- to address now, and then have a framework agreement under which the governments could negotiate additional mutual recognition on a sectoral basis at a later time.

Overall, in my view, prospects for a quick and economically significant US - UK trade deal that focuses on these core trade issues are fairly good. A successful negotiation here would be the first positive step forward for trade liberalization in quite some time, and could generate momentum for liberalization more broadly.

Thank you for your time, and I look forward to answering your questions.

———————

Mr. POE. The gentleman yields back.

And, Dr. Hamilton, you are recognized for 5 minutes.

STATEMENT OF DANIEL S. HAMILTON, PH.D., EXECUTIVE DIRECTOR, CENTER FOR TRANSATLANTIC RELATIONS, JOHNS HOPKINS SCHOOL OF ADVANCED AND INTERNATIONAL STUDIES

Mr. HAMILTON. Thank you, Mr. Chairman, distinguished members of the committee, if I could also submit my testimony to the record.

I would just like to indicate I have two appendices in the testimony that try to provide the latest data on jobs, trade, and investment between not only the United States and Europe, but most of the States here represented by members of the subcommittee. This is the latest data. We have an annual survey on the transatlantic economy. So maybe it is of some interest.

It affirms what the members of the committee said at the beginning. Mr. Chairman, we estimate, if you take indirect and direct jobs together, it is about 1 million Texas jobs related to commerce with Europe. And the U.K. is the number one source of onshore jobs in Texas.

Mr. Rohrabacher, and the other California delegates, about 1.2 million California jobs directly and indirectly related to commerce with Europe. Again, the U.K. a major source of that.

Mr. Keating, for Massachusetts, about 450,000 jobs in Massachusetts directly or indirectly related to this. And the U.K., again, the number one source of onshore jobs in Massachusetts.

And for the Congressmen from New York, Congressman Meeks and others, also about 1 million jobs put together, roughly estimated, and again, the U.K. the number one source of onshore jobs.

So the data does tell us that a trade and investment arrangement, when the U.K. leaves the EU, is absolutely in the interest of the United States and to the U.K. But my basic message is such an agreement will do even more for our economies if it is embedded in a broader North Atlantic initiative for jobs and growth with our closest allies. Because the rest of Europe also provides not only as much but actually more jobs, trade, and investment to each of our States.

And we should avoid a false choice between three points of the transatlantic stool, if you will, between the U.S. the U.K., the U.S. and the EU, and the U.K. and the EU. Each of those stools have to be strong and sturdy when we all face intensified winds of global competition. We cannot afford to let ourselves, you know, fall in between the cracks of that or open up false alternatives.

Back to those numbers again, in Texas and in New York, for instance, two thirds of the jobs to both of those States actually come from the rest of Europe. And three-quarters of those jobs in—I am sorry—in Massachusetts and in California come from the rest of Europe. So the U.K. is important, but the rest of Europe provides even more to all of us. We have to make sure we do this in a simultaneous way.

Much of the reason why American companies are invested in the U.K. is because of the access it brings them to the European market. American companies based in the U.K. export more to the rest of Europe than American companies based in China export to the rest of the world. And so a major motivation of our companies is to understand how the U.K.-EU relationship will work and what is our position on that as we move forward with the U.K. itself.

So just a bit of point on process. As Mr. Lester said, the U.K. has to negotiate a number of things here. And it is likely, frankly, that it will be about 6 years before the U.K. and the EU have a new type of trade agreement beyond Brexit. So we need to orient ourselves to a different type of time scale. I don't mean not starting the conversations as Dr. Gardiner said. I think we can explore them. I think you can in fact get a framework in place. But we should be attune to the dynamic here.

We should understand the U.K. sells twice as much to the EU in goods and services as does the United States. So it will absolutely be looking at what this relationship will be. But what would be the parameters of a deal? I agree with Mr. Lester that it is not just about trade. Trade is not the driver of our relationship with the U.K. or with Europe. It is investment. That is what drives everything. And so it must be a broader arrangement than just a trade deal.

Because actually trade tariffs across the Atlantic, traditional things, are pretty low. That actually is going to get done, somebody said, on a weekend. It is not going to be a tough part of it. The real advantage and where we can really open up opportunity is in other areas. Services. We are each other's most important services markets. That is where the jobs are. That is with sleeping giant of the transatlantic economy. Because there are so many barriers. It is a huge strength to the United States as well as the EU.

Regulatory procedures, it is not about convincing one side to take the other's procedures about how can we align them and conform them and recognize each other.

And the last point is to take the global system forward. We can pioneer standards that are not like bringing Vietnam or other countries up to some standards, but taking two high-standard entities and taking the rest of the world with them by establishing a high bar for the way we can conduct our commerce. That is a broad package we can conduct with the U.K. But we must do something very similar with the rest of our allies in Europe.

And if we can do that together in a mutually reinforcing way, I think we will all advance better and it will be a North Atlantic project in which the U.K. will continue to play a major and important role.

Thank you.

[The prepared statement of Mr. Hamilton follows:]

JOHNS HOPKINS
SCHOOL *of* ADVANCED
INTERNATIONAL STUDIES

**Next Steps in the 'Special Relationship' –
Impact of a US-UK Free Trade Agreement**

Testimony by
Dr. Daniel S. Hamilton
Austrian Marshall Plan Foundation Professor
Executive Director, Center for Transatlantic Relations
Johns Hopkins University SAIS

Joint Hearing by the
Subcommittee on Terrorism, Non-Proliferation and Trade
Subcommittee on Europe, Eurasia and Emerging Threats
of the
Committee on Foreign Affairs
U.S. House of Representatives

February 1, 2017

Distinguished Members of the Committee,

Thank you for the opportunity to speak with you today.

A trade and investment agreement between the United States and the United Kingdom will be vital to each of our countries once the UK leaves the European Union (EU) under the process known as 'Brexit.' But such an agreement will do even more to advance the interests of both parties if embedded in a broader North Atlantic Initiative for Jobs and Growth so we and our allies are better positioned to advance both our economic and our strategic interests in a world of intensified global competition.

As Brexit unfolds, the United States has a vital stake in ensuring that each point in the transatlantic triangle -- U.S.-UK, UK-EU, and U.S.-Europe -- is strong and sturdy. Failure to ensure that these three elements are mutually reinforcing rather than mutually disruptive will shortchange American workers, American consumers, American companies, and American interests.

How is Brexit Likely to Unfold?

British Prime Minister Theresa May has made it clear that her government intends to take the UK out of the European Union (EU) and to end its participation in the EU's Single Market for goods, services, people and capital as well as from the customs union for goods. She will not pursue partial or associate EU membership, nor will she seek special arrangements similar to those Norway and Switzerland have with the EU.

In March 2017 Prime Minister May plans to declare formally that the UK intends to leave the EU, triggering Article 50 of the Treaty on the European Union, which provides for a two-year

process to negotiate the terms of separation. There is an option to extend this timeline if the UK and all 27 remaining member states of the European Union agree, but the goal is to have the UK leave the EU by April 2019.

UK-EU 'exit' negotiations will focus on resolving such legacy issues as budget commitments. Approval requires a qualified majority among the remaining EU 27 governments. When the UK exits the EU, the UK government's Great Reform Bill will transform EU legislation into UK legislation. That will ensure initial consistency with current rules in the UK. But once the UK does leave the EU, it will assess whether it wants to continue with those EU-oriented rules or whether it wants to determine, and then implement, new and different regulations.

Brexit and the UK's Trading Relationships

When the UK exits the EU it will also have to do three things that will affect U.S. economic interests.

First, it will have to replace the EU's common external tariff with its own customs tariff, and will also need to submit new tariff commitments for both goods and services at the World Trade Organization (WTO).

Second, it will negotiate new trade arrangements between the UK and the EU 27.

Third, it will want to negotiate new trade arrangements with the United States as well as many other non-EU countries.

The UK and the WTO

Currently, the EU makes collective commitments for its members, including the UK, when it comes to tariffs for goods and services at the WTO. When the UK leaves the EU it will need to either replicate or distinguish its own commitments from those of the EU. It is unlikely to simply replicate EU commitments, for instance in agriculture or services, and so will need to set forth different commitments. These commitments must be agreed by consensus among the entire WTO membership -- 161 countries. If only one WTO member objects, the UK's schedule of commitments will be disqualified. The EU itself could block it. Russia could block it. China or India could block it.

Knowing this, the UK is likely to face a series of pre-negotiations with a variety of countries before it sets its new WTO schedule of commitments. Some countries may be reasonable, others may seek to gain advantage at UK expense. All of this will take some time and preoccupy the UK's limited bench of trade negotiators.

The United States will be particularly keen to know how far the UK will be prepared to go in such areas as services or agriculture when it comes to trade with other WTO members. Until the UK's WTO commitments are known and agreed, our trade negotiators will not know the baseline for their own bilateral negotiations with the UK.

The UK and the EU

Since the UK government does not seek to maintain its participation in the EU's Single Market, it will seek to negotiate a new trade and investment agreement with the European Union. A new trading relationship between the UK and the EU will need to be approved by parliaments of all 28 current EU member states and by the European Parliament. Given the complicated issues and procedures involved, it is likely that such a new agreement would only take effect sometime in the middle of the next decade.

This means there is likely to be a period of transition that could last as much as six years. Both parties will also have to negotiate trade and commercial arrangements for this transitional period. Such arrangements will not be subject to parliamentary approval.

A future UK-EU trade arrangement is unlikely to simply replicate the status quo in terms of UK access to the Single Market. The terms are likely to be less advantageous than if the UK were a member of the EU. While tariff-free access for goods is likely, firms based in the UK are likely to face some local content requirements within the EU. It is unlikely that there will be tariff-free access for services. UK financial services in particular are likely to lose their current right to "passport" financial services to the rest of the EU. Each of these provisions -- as well as related provisions to be negotiated during the transition period -- are likely to affect U.S. companies and banks with affiliates in the UK.

What do these developments mean for the United States and a U.S.-UK deal?

First, EU rules mean that London cannot legally begin negotiating a trade deal with Washington before the UK leaves the EU, which at the earliest will be March 2019. When Washington sets out to negotiate a formal bilateral deal with the UK, it will want to understand the UK's new WTO commitments and the nature of UK-EU transitional arrangements following Brexit, as well as London's end goals with regard to a deal with the UK's largest trade partner, the EU. This will all take time.

Washington and London can, however, move ahead now with two types of discussions. Initially, the two sides intend to start on what the White House and the Prime Minister's office are calling a "trade negotiation agreement" that identifies potential stumbling blocks and scopes what could be done before the UK leaves the EU. Based on these discussions, US-UK "shadow" negotiations could create a basic framework for an agreement once such an agreement can be negotiated officially, and to understand how UK-EU arrangements would also affect US-UK considerations during what may be a six-year transitional period. That would mean getting a jump start on the negotiations while respecting the Article 50 and WTO processes.

Since Congress has purview over commerce, and Trade Promotion Authority (TPA) authority provided by the Congress faces renewal before this timeline plays itself out, it will be important for the Congress to be part of this process.

26

Issues in a U.S.-UK Negotiation

The United Kingdom is a critical economic partner for the United States, and the U.S. should ensure that bilateral ties are strengthened, rather than disrupted, by Brexit. But Europe -- even without the UK -- remains America's largest trading partner, greatest source of foreign investment, and largest source of onshored jobs.

In **Appendix 1** I offer various data that explain America's stake in healthy commerce with the UK and Europe.

The data underscore a basic point: United States has a vital interest in strengthening and modernizing its ties not only with the UK, but with its other European allies and partners as well, and not getting trapped into a false choice between the two. As the Brexit process proceeds, the U.S. must ensure that U.S. workers, consumers and companies do not get caught in any cracks that may appear as the UK and the EU, the UK and the U.S., and the U.S. and the EU all adjust to post-Brexit realities. The United States has a vested interest in ensuring that each leg of this transatlantic stool remains strong and sturdy, particularly as the winds of global competition intensify.

America's significant commercial and financial presence in the UK is premised in large part on UK membership in the European Union -- the largest, wealthiest and most important foreign market in the world to U.S. companies. For decades, the UK has served as a strategic gateway to the European Union for U.S. firms and financial institutions. The primary motivation of many U.S. companies to invest in the UK has not been to serve only the UK market but to gain access to the much bigger EU Single Market. Similarly, many U.S. banks and financial institutions have relied on "passporting" via London to access the Single Market. U.S. affiliates based in the UK export more to the rest of Europe, in fact, than U.S. affiliates based in China export to the rest of the world.

Just as the U.S. has an interest in ensuring that Brexit does not damage its strong commercial interests with other European countries, so too does the United Kingdom. The UK exports almost half of its goods and services to the EU -- twice as much as to the U.S.

In short, as the UK and the U.S. pursue their exploratory discussions over a new set of economic arrangements, each is likely to have its own economic relationship with the EU in mind. Since many U.S. companies are based in the UK because of its role as a gateway to the Single Market, U.S. negotiators will want to know how open, wide and strong that gateway will be after Brexit. And while the UK will want to move quickly ahead with a deal with the U.S., it is also likely to condition its efforts on the nature of its parallel negotiations with the EU.

What would be the major issues in a U.S.-UK deal? Agreeing on reductions in traditional trade tariffs is not likely to be very troublesome, since most tariffs are already quite small, with a few notable exceptions, such as agriculture. The much bigger gains from a bilateral deal would come from

- reducing barriers to services, the "sleeping giant" of the transatlantic economy and where job gains are likely to occur;

JOHNS HOPKINS
SCHOOL of ADVANCED
INTERNATIONAL STUDIES

▣ recognizing that various regulatory procedures in one country essentially conform or are equivalent to those in the other country;

▣ pioneering standards in new economic areas that could push the global frontier.

Keeping in mind that in each of this tracks both the U.S. and the UK have more to gain from achieving some agreement with the EU than simply with each other, each will want to ensure that whatever agreements they reach with each other serve to strengthen, rather than disrupt, their more significant commercial connections with the EU. Similarly, the EU will want to ensure that a U.S.-UK agreement, as well as any separate arrangements it may advance with the U.S. and with the UK, will enhance its own economic ties with two of its most significant economic partners.

The intertwined nature of UK-EU, US-UK, and US-EU negotiations can be best understood by looking at financial services. When the UK leaves the EU, financial services institutions based in the UK will lose their "passport" to provide services across the Single Market. This will not only disrupt the UK financial services industry. Many U.S. banks and other financial services companies established a presence in the UK to take advantage of passporting via the City of London to access the Single Market. Unless similar provisions are incorporated in any new UK-EU arrangements, many of these U.S. firms will probably choose another entry point to access the Single Market in the future. This will make a huge difference with regard to London's role as a financial hub, may accelerate the rise of other European financial centers, for instance Frankfurt, and will reinforce U.S. interest in strong and predictable financial services procedures with the EU. It will also affect the U.S. approach to financial services in any U.S.-UK arrangement. The EU has established an "equivalence" regime that extends limited access rights to non-EU countries, such as the U.S., that have rules that have been deemed "equivalent," but this is a relatively new and somewhat inconsistent approach with rights that are weaker than those granted under full "passporting.

With these considerations in mind, U.S.-UK discussions could productively focus on three lines of discussion/negotiation: market access, regulatory cooperation, and 'rules'.

▣ Market access discussions would focus on goods trade and customs duties; services trade; public procurement; and clear, simple and aligned rules of origin.

▣ Discussions regarding regulatory cooperation would address issues of regulatory coherence; technical barriers to trade; sanitary and phytosanitary questions; and good practice in a range of sectors, from medical devices and chemicals to vehicles, pharmaceuticals, and financial services.

▣ Discussions of "rules" could encompass such issues as intellectual property, digital trade, or state-owned enterprises that could create standards as orientation for many other countries around the world.

A U.S-UK agreement could be harder than some anticipate. Disagreements are likely to arise over differences in regulatory policy. Issues such as public procurement and healthcare have

strong public constituencies and are often extremely sensitive. Remaining tariff barriers, especially in agriculture, often reflect the most politically difficult cases. It is unclear, for instance, whether UK farmers will be keen on a trade deal that would open them up to U.S. competition at the very time they are losing generous EU subsidies, or whether they will be willing to accommodate U.S. interests in changing their rules related to hygiene or genetically-modified organisms if that makes it harder for them to sell to the EU, which is their largest market.

The benefits, however, could be considerable, and important to many constituencies across the United States. **In Appendix 2** I offer data underscoring the significance of UK/European-sourced jobs, trade and investment for each state represented by Members of the two Subcommittees hosting this hearing today.

U.S.-UK discussions along the three lines I have outlined would be compatible with the way the UK is likely to conduct its relations with the EU, and would be similar to how the U.S. and the EU have been conducting their own negotiations. In sum, this three-track framework (market access, regulatory cooperation with individual sectoral agreements, rules) could offer common orientation at each point of the transatlantic triangle -- U.S.-UK, UK-EU, and U.S.-EU.

A North Atlantic Initiative for Jobs and Growth

This means that the U.S. should champion a multi-channel transatlantic economic initiative -- a North Atlantic Initiative for Jobs and Growth -- that generates synergies rather than competition among a new U.S.-UK economic relationship and both post-Brexit UK-EU and U.S.-European ties. As the U.S. and UK move forward with their own discussions, the U.S. should also move ahead with a new agenda with its own European allies and partners as well.

An immediate revival of the U.S.-EU Transatlantic Trade and Investment Partnership (TTIP) is unlikely, given the advent of a new U.S. Administration and a series of important European elections in 2017. But at an early date the U.S. and the EU could issue a political statement affirming the value of transatlantic economic ties and a mutual commitment to strengthen the transatlantic economy, and use the Transatlantic Economic Council to move forward in areas where progress has already been registered or is likely.

A multi-channel transatlantic economic initiative that generates synergies rather than competition between a U.S.-UK trade agreement and both post-Brexit UK-EU and U.S.-European ties is ambitious. It will be tough to manage and conclude. But the potential payoff is high, and the geostrategic impact of such an initiative could be as profound as the direct economic benefits.

Such an initiative promises to be an operational reflection of basic values we share with our European partners as democratic societies rooted in respect for human rights and the rule of law. The UK and our other European allies are more likely to have greater faith in America's security commitments if they are anchored by strong trade and investment links. A strong multi-channel transatlantic initiative would also reassure Americans that the post-Brexit UK as well as the post-Brexit European Union are each committed to look outward rather than inward. In a world of rising powers and intensified competition, it could ensure that Europeans and Americans

continue as rule-makers instead of becoming rule-takers. Standards negotiated among the U.S., UK and our other European allies are almost certainly to be better for American workers, consumers and companies than comparable rules found in the WTO. Agreement on such issues as intellectual property, services, digital trade, and tackling discriminatory regulations would set the global standard.

Now that the British government has decided to exit the European Union, the United States has a vital interest in ensuring that Brexit is a success for Great Britain, Europe, and the transatlantic partnership. A "Global Britain" that retains and deepens its strong economic links to the United States and to continental Europe, is outward-looking and has a robust economy ready to shoulder a greater British contribution to our common defense and to address global challenges together with us is a Britain that Americans can and should support. A "Global Britain" that is isolated from the United States and its key European partners, that seeks to stake out its own positions on global issues without regard to its strong transatlantic links, is likely to be a lonely and increasingly impoverished Britain unable to be a value-added partner to America.

Similarly, a messy and acrimonious divorce between the UK and our European allies and partners would not only disrupt U.S. jobs, trade and investment, it would impair the ability of our major allies to deal with a whole host of challenges important to the United States -- generating inclusive economic growth, fighting terrorism, addressing destabilizing flows of people, and fighting threats in many other world regions.

It is decidedly in U.S. interests to ensure that Brexit serves to strengthen, rather than weaken, our transatlantic alliance.

*   *   *

JOHNS HOPKINS
SCHOOL *of* ADVANCED
INTERNATIONAL STUDIES

Appendix 1[1]

America's Economic Stake in Healthy Commerce with Britain and Europe

The United Kingdom is a critical economic partner for the United States. Bilateral trade flows are strong. In 2015 the United States exported $124.5 billion in goods and services to the UK, and imported $121 billion worth of British goods and services. The United States is Britain's largest export destination after the EU.

U.S.-UK trade is significant. But the real driver of the British-American economy is investment. In 2015, U.S. foreign direct investment in the UK totaled a record $593.0 billion and UK foreign direct investment in the U.S. totaled $483.8 billion. Estimated sales of American and British affiliates totaled more than $1.3 trillion. The UK accounted for 22% of overall global U.S. investment outside the United States. U.S. investment flows to the UK rose by nearly 30% in the first nine months of 2016. UK affiliates domiciled in the United States improved the U.S. trade balance by exporting $74 billion worth of goods from the U.S. in 2014.

U.S. affiliates employed almost 1.4 million workers in the UK while UK affiliates employed roughly 1.1 million Americans, according to 2015 estimates. British firms were the #1 source of onshored jobs in 25 of the 50 U.S. states in 2014.

America's capital stock in the UK is more than double combined U.S. investment in South America, the Middle East and Africa. Total U.S. investment stock in China was just 11% of the comparable figure in the United Kingdom in 2014. Even when the U.S. investment position of China and India are combined—roughly $94 billion in 2014—the figure is just 16% of total U.S. investment in the United Kingdom (Chart 1).

Chart 1: America's Preference for the UK vs. China and India.

(U.S. direct investment position,* billions of $)

*U.S. Foreign Direct Investment (stock).

Source: Bureau of Economic Analysis.

Data as of February 2016.

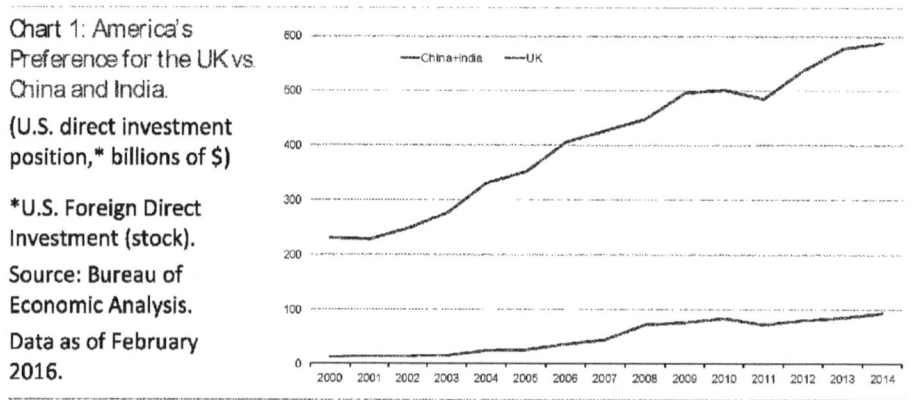

---

[1] Figures are drawn from Daniel S. Hamilton and Joseph P. Quinlan, *The Transatlantic Economy 2017: Annual Survey of Jobs, Trade and Investment between the United States and Europe* (Washington, DC: Center for Transatlantic Relations, 2017).

31

JOHNS HOPKINS
SCHOOL of ADVANCED
INTERNATIONAL STUDIES

In sum, the UK and the U.S. are critical partners for each other. Wealthy consumers, respect for the rule of law, the ease of doing business, credible institutions, and, importantly, **membership to the European Union** have long made the UK a more attractive place to do business for American firms than either China or India.

Whatever the metric—total assets, R&D expenditures, foreign affiliate sales and even affiliate employment—the United Kingdom is a key pillar of America's global economic infrastructure and a key hub for the global competitiveness of U.S. firms. Since 2000, the U.K. has accounted for nearly 9% of the cumulative global income of U.S. affiliates, a proxy for global earnings. The UK ranks number one in the world in terms of U.S. foreign affiliate value added (or output). The output of U.S. affiliates in the UK totaled $153 billion in 2013, about the same as the entire GDP of Vietnam or Ukraine (Chart 2). U.S. affiliates in the UK produced three times more than U.S. affiliates in China.

Chart 2: Operations of U.S. Foreign Affiliates in the UK *	Billions of $	% of Global Total	Rank
Total Assets	4,982	22%	1
Value Added (Output of Affiliates)	153	11%	1
R&D	5	11%	2
Capital Expenditures	19	8%	2
Foreign Affiliate Sales	643	11%	2
Employment (thousands of employees)	1,233	10%	2
Manufacturing (thousands of employees)	300	6%	5

*Data for majority-owned foreign affiliates, 2012.

Source: Bureau of Economic Analysis.

Data as of February 2016.

U.S. affiliate exports from the UK still totaled over $190 billion in 2013, the last year of available data. That figure is more than double U.S. affiliate exports from Mexico and nearly four times greater than U.S. affiliate exports from China—two lower-cost nations more closely associated with U.S. affiliate exports. U.S. affiliate exports from the UK each year are greater than the total exports of most nations.

The U.S. Stake in Healthy Commerce with Europe, Even after Brexit

As these figures show, the U.S.-UK commercial relationship is among the most deeply connected in the world. But it is important to place the U.S.-UK relationship in the broader context of U.S. economic relations with our other European allies and partners.

The EU Single Market will remain the major destination for American goods, services and investments, even if the UK is not part of it. In nominal U.S. dollar terms, the European Union (plus Norway, Switzerland, Iceland) accounted for 23.4% of world output in 2016 according to estimates from the International Monetary Fund. Even when the United Kingdom is excluded from the figures, the EU's aggregate output—$14.9 trillion, or 19.8%—is among the largest in the world, less than America's share (24.7%), but in excess of China's—15.1%. Based on purchasing power parity figures, the European Union's share was greater than that of the United States, but slightly less than China's in 2016.

U.S. companies still see Europe as a major hub for their global operations. Europe accounted for nearly 70% of total U.S. FDI outflows in 2016. The Asia-Pacific region represented just 21% of the total, underscoring the bias and preference among U.S. firms for Europe versus Asia. In 2016 we estimate that U.S. FDI outflows to Europe totaled $220 billion, a 12% rise from the levels of 2015 ($196 billion). U.S. investment in the UK, while significant, accounted for just 22% of the total. 78% went to other European countries.

Despite all the hype about rising powers and emerging markets, Europe remains the most important commercial market in the world for the United States and the major geo-economic base for U.S. companies. That base is enhanced if the UK is included, but Europe retains its preeminent importance for the United States even without the UK. None of America's other commercial arteries are as integrated. The $5.5. trillion transatlantic economy is the fulcrum of the global economy, generating 15 million jobs on both sides of the Atlantic.

Europe -- even without the UK -- remains America's largest trading partner, greatest source of foreign investment, and largest source of onshored jobs.

Massachusetts, New Jersey and Florida each export 8 times more to Europe than to China. New York exports 7 times more to Europe than to China. Indiana exports 7 times more to Europe than to China. Texas exports 3 times more to Europe than to China, and California exports twice as much to Europe as to China.

American affiliates of European companies also generate U.S. exports -- $230 billion in 2014, 32 UK affiliates in America were responsible for close to one-third of those exports, but the remaining two-thirds were generated by other U.S.-based European affiliates. In the end, the more European affiliates export from the U.S., the higher the number of U.S. jobs and the greater U.S. export figures.

US companies invest twice as much in Europe as in all of the Asia-Pacific region. In 2016 Europe accounted for an estimated 72% percent of all investment flowing into the United States from foreign shores. Europe invests four times as much in America than does Asia. The UK leads the way, with $493 billion invested in 2015, but Luxembourg, the Netherlands, Switzerland, Germany and France invested $1.255 *trillion*. That reflects the strategy of European firms to be "inside" the United States -- the world's largest and most dynamic market.

One of the greatest benefits of this presence is the creation of U.S. jobs. Europe is by far the largest source of "onshored" jobs in the United States. Chart 3 provides a snapshot of state employment provided directly by UK and other European affiliates on the ground across the United States.

JOHNS HOPKINS
SCHOOL of ADVANCED
INTERNATIONAL STUDIES

Chart 3. Top 20 States by Jobs Supported
Directly by European/UK Investment, 2014
(Thousands of employees)

U.S. State	Europe w/o UK	*UK*	Total Europe/UK
California	295.6	*98.2*	**393.8**
Texas	224.0	*107.2*	**331.2**
New York	206.8	*103.7*	**310.5**
Pennsylvania	162.8	*60.1*	**222.9**
Illinois	135.8	*59.3*	**195.1**
New Jersey	134.5	*40.0*	**174.5**
Florida	122.9	*51.4*	**174.3**
North Carolina	140.1	*34.0*	**174.1**
Massachusetts	123.2	*40.6*	**163.8**
Ohio	105.5	*42.1*	**147.6**
Michigan	117.9	*24.0*	**141.9**
Virginia	99.8	*31.9*	**131.7**
Georgia	100.9	*29.0*	**129.9**
Indiana	64.3	*31.8*	**96.1**
South Carolina	82.9	*11.9*	**94.8**
Maryland	63.3	*20.4*	**83.7**
Tennessee	60.9	*20.2*	**81.1**
Connecticut	60.9	*20.0*	**80.9**
Missouri	49.6	*23.1*	**72.7**
Minnesota	48.4	*16.8*	**65.2**

The charts underestimate the true impact on US jobs of America's commercial ties to UK/Europe in at least two ways. First, jobs tied to exports and imports of goods and services are not included. Second, many other jobs are created indirectly through suppliers or distribution networks and related activities.

Appendix 2[2]

UK- and European-Sourced Jobs, Trade and Investment in U.S. States Represented by Subcommittee Members

California

- Roughly 1.2 million jobs in California are directly or indirectly related to California's commerce with Europe.
- 394,000 California jobs are directly supported by European investment.
- The UK follows Japan as the top source of onshored jobs in California, accounting for 98,200 jobs -- a quarter of all California jobs onshored from Europe. Germany, Switzerland and France accounted for an additional 205,900 jobs.
- California exported $33.1 billion to Europe in 2015 -- almost 2 1/2 times the amount that California exports to China.
- In 2015 California was the #1 U.S. state exporting to Europe, and in 2014 it was the #1 state profiting from onshored jobs from Europe. The UK is the third largest European market for California goods, trailing the Netherlands and Germany.

Florida

- Over 500,000 Florida jobs are directly or indirectly related to the state's commerce with Europe.
- 174,300 Florida jobs are directly supported by European investment.
- The UK ranks as the largest source of onshored jobs in Florida, accounting for 51,400 jobs. France and Germany accounted for 54,500 jobs.
- Florida exported $9 billion to Europe in 2015 -- almost 9 times the amount that Florida exports to China.
- In 2015 Florida was the 12th largest U.S. state exporting to Europe, and in 2014 it hosted the 7th largest number of onshored jobs from Europe.
- Germany is the largest European market for Florida goods, followed by Switzerland, and then the UK. The Netherlands and France round out the top 5.

Massachusetts

- Close to 450,000 jobs in Massachusetts are directly or indirectly related to the state's commerce with Europe.
- Massachusetts jobs directly supported by European investment have risen 37% since 2006.
- The UK is the #1 source of onshored jobs in Massachusetts, accounting directly for 40,600 jobs -- one-fourth of all onshored jobs in the state. The Netherlands, France and Germany accounted for an additional 83,000 jobs.
- The EU accounts for 45% of global investment in Massachusetts and 43% of global investment in Boston.

[2] Figures are drawn from Daniel S. Hamilton and Joseph P. Quinlan, *The Transatlantic Economy 2017: Annual Survey of Jobs, Trade and Investment between the United States and Europe* (Washington, DC: Center for Transatlantic Relations, 2017).

- Massachusetts exported goods valued at 9.5 billion to Europe in 2015 -- 8 times more than to China.
- The UK is the top European export market for Massachusetts. But Massachusetts exports to the UK totaled $1.2 billion, ranking it third as a European export market behind Germany and the Netherlands.

New York

- Slightly less than 1 million New York jobs are directly or indirectly related to New York's commerce with Europe.
- 310,500 New York jobs are directly supported by European investment.
- The UK ranks as the top source of onshored jobs in New York, accounting for 103,700 jobs -- about a third of all New York jobs onshored from Europe. Switzerland and France accounted for an additional 89,600 jobs.
- New York exported $28.2 billion to Europe in 2015 -- over 8 times the amount the state exports to China.
- In 2015 New York was the third largest U.S. state exporter to Europe, and in 2014 it hosted the third largest number of onshored jobs from Europe.
- Switzerland is the largest European market for New York goods, followed by the UK, Belgium, Germany and France.

Pennsylvania

- Close to 675,000 Pennsylvania jobs are directly or indirectly related to Pennsylvania's commerce with Europe.
- 222,900 Pennsylvania jobs are directly supported by European investment - 22% more than in 2006.
- The UK ranks as the largest source of onshored jobs in Pennsylvania, accounting for 60,100 jobs. But the Netherlands, Germany and France accounted for 107,900 jobs.
- Pennsylvania exported $10.5 billion to Europe -- 5 times the amount that Pennsylvania exports to China.
- In 2015 Pennsylvania was the 7th largest U.S. state exporting to Europe, and in 2014 it hosted the 4th largest number of onshored jobs from Europe.
- The UK is the largest European market for Pennsylvania goods, followed by Germany, the Netherlands, Belgium and France.

South Carolina

- Roughly 285,000 jobs in South Carolina are directly or indirectly related to South Carolina 's commerce with Europe.
- 94,800 South Carolina jobs are directly supported by European investment -- 12% more than in 2006.
- The UK ranks as the fourth largest source of onshored jobs in South Carolina, accounting for 11,900 jobs. But Germany accounted for 25,800 jobs, and France for 19,300.
- South Carolina exported $9.8 billion to Europe in 2015 -- twice the amount that South Carolina exports to China. Many of South Carolina's exports to China come from European

companies at home in the state. BMW, for instance, domiciled in South Carolina, is the largest U.S. exporter of cars by value to the rest of the world.

- In 2015 South Carolina was the 8th largest U.S. state exporting to Europe.
- Germany is the largest European market for South Carolina goods, followed by the UK, Belgium, France and the Netherlands.

Texas

- Slightly less than 1 million Texas jobs are directly or indirectly related to the state's commerce with Europe.
- 331,200 Texas jobs are directly supported by European investment -- over 40% more than in 2006.
- The UK ranks as the largest source of onshored jobs in Texas, accounting for 107,200 jobs. France and Germany accounted for 89,000 jobs.
- Texas exported $31.9 billion to Europe in 2015 -- almost 3 times the amount that Texas exports to China.
- In 2015 Texas was the #2 U.S. state exporting to Europe, and in 2014 it hosted the 2nd largest number of jobs onshored from Europe.
- The Netherlands is the largest European market for Texas goods, followed by Belgium, and then the UK. Germany and France round out the top 5.

Virginia

- Close to 400,000 Virginia jobs are directly or indirectly related to the state's commerce with Europe.
- 131,700 Virginia jobs are directly supported by European investment in the state -- over 17% more than in 2006.
- The UK ranks as the largest source of onshored jobs in Virginia, accounting for 31,900 jobs. The Netherlands, France and Germany accounted for 46,600 jobs.
- Virginia exported $5 billion to Europe in 2015 -- about 3 times the amount that Virginia exports to China.
- In 2014 Virginia hosted the 12th largest number of onshored jobs from Europe.
- The UK is the largest European market for Virginia goods, followed by Germany, Belgium, the Netherlands and Italy.

Wisconsin

- Roughly 150,000 Wisconsin jobs are directly or indirectly related to Wisconsin's commerce with Europe.
- 57,500 Wisconsin jobs are directly supported by European investment in the state.
- The UK ranks as the largest European source of onshored jobs in Wisconsin, accounting for 13,100 jobs. Germany, Switzerland and France accounted for 25,000 jobs.
- Wisconsin exported $4.2 billion to Europe in 2015 -- almost 3 times the amount that Wisconsin exports to China.
- The UK is the largest European market for Wisconsin goods, followed by Germany, France, Belgium and the Netherlands.

Mr. POE. Thank you, Dr. Hamilton.

The Chair recognizes itself for questioning for 5 minutes.

Thank all of you for your testimony. It seems to me that, I agree with you, Dr. Hamilton, that just because the United States and the United Kingdom are working on a trade deal doesn't exclude the European Union on working with them from the U.K.'s point of view or from the United States' point of view.

It just seems to me, though, also that this trade deal is something that we should move forward too for all of the reasons all of the members have said at some point. A couple of you mentioned that there are some issues dealing with the fact that the United Kingdom is still part of the European Union and hasn't really exited yet. There is kind of a limbo land.

What procedures are in play to limit what we can do regarding the fact that Brexit is still not done yet? So what are some of the sticking points between the relationship between the United Kingdom and the European Union during this limbo time? Dr. Hamilton?

Mr. HAMILTON. Well, and this was mentioned, they have to trigger what is called article 50 of the European Treaty. So they have not yet done that. They anticipate doing it in March. It has a 2-year timeline in which they could then negotiate their exit, if you will. But if they all agree that the timeline should be extended because they are not done, they can do that.

So we should orient ourselves to March 2019 as the starting point. It is likely the U.K. Government, at that point, would probably, with one bill, say all existing EU legislation that is now currently in the U.K. will be U.K. legislation. They can change it after that, but that will be the baseline.

At the same time, the U.K. has to do three other important things. One, it has to give the World Trade Organization, of which it would then be a member, a new set of commitments on goods and services, tariffs, and all sorts of things like that that it doesn't do now because it is part of EU. That has to receive unanimous consent by all members of the World Trade Organization. Let that sink in for a minute. The EU itself could block that. China could block it. Russia could block it. Anybody disgruntled. India could block it. So that will force the U.K. to have also pre-negotiations with the whole set of countries to make sure that that moves slowly. But that is going to take some time.

The second thing it must do is then negotiate a free trade agreement or some sort of trade and investment agreement with the European Union itself. That is what I mentioned. That, I believe, will take 6 years. And it will arrange probably for a transition period, then, with the EU that does not, at the moment, require Parliamentary approval, to sort out their arrangements. So as you said, it will be a little twilight zone, but it will I think the twilight zone will extend for some years.

And then third, it has to negotiate new agreements with everybody else; the United States, all other non-EU countries. So it will be very preoccupied with how it does that. And so I think we should have this timeline in mind and use the timeline to our advantage.

So there is nothing wrong with starting, as Dr. Gardiner said, these kinds of exploratory discussions to find where the stumbling blocks are, the problems, and the issues. One could even move then to almost a shadow negotiation that could set up and tee up a U.S.-U.K. framework so that when we would be ready and the U.K. is able, we could then move quickly.

Mr. POE. All right. Dr. Hamilton, I am going to reclaim my time. Let me reclaim my time.

You have lost me on the number of years. Starting with March of this year, how long is it going to take before—approximately, how long is it going to take before there could actually be a negotiation between the United States and the United Kingdom on a bilateral trade? Approximately.

Mr. HAMILTON. Formal negotiation could happen as soon as they leave the EU. So in 2 years. They are unlikely to want to finalize a deal with the United States unless they understand what the EU dimension is of their trade since that is actually their major partner.

So my estimate told, to implement both of those, is 8 years.

Mr. POE. Okay. Dr. Gardiner, do you want to weigh in on that?

Turn your microphone on.

Mr. GARDINER. Yes. I would like to respond too to that.

Firstly, with regard to the amount of time it would take Britain to negotiate a trade agreement with the European Union, that is not going to take 6 years. I believe that deal will be conducted very, very swiftly. It is in the EU's interest to have a good trade agreement with the United Kingdom. The United Kingdom, of course, is a very, very powerful economy. The world's fifth biggest economy. It is going to overtake Germany by 2030 as Europe's largest economy. It is not in the EU's interest to delay a deal with the United Kingdom. I would expect that deal will be struck within this 2-year period before Britain exits the European Union.

Secondly, I would point out that, you know, the United Kingdom can begin negotiating a trade agreement with the United States now. They do not have to wait before Britain exits the European Union. You cannot of course implement such a deal until Britain leaves the EU in March 2019. But you can do all of the discussions and negotiations ahead of Britain's exit.

So those discussions can already begin. And there is nothing to stop Great Britain from doing that. So that is a very important——

Mr. POE. Thank you, Dr. Gardiner. My time has expired. Thank you.

The Chair recognizes the gentleman from Massachusetts, ranking member, Mr. Keating.

Mr. KEATING. Thank you, Mr. Chairman. American trade with the U.K. represents one-fifth of the trade with the European Union as a whole. The other four-fifths deals with the rest of the European countries, including Germany, our largest EU trading partner. So moving ahead on this, and I think it is unsettled, Mr. Gardiner, whether or not legally that can be done. Clearly it is unsettled. I won't say one way or the other.

But moving ahead bilaterally, the message it sends to the rest of the EU, which is 80 percent of our trade that is left, plus the message it sends politically, and let's face it, trade deals are political, is the wrong message. So I am not saying one excludes the other, as I said in my opening remarks. But there is a danger in having a prioritized bilateral agreement and leaving the rest of Europe by the side, including allies like Germany. I would like Mr. Hamilton to comment on that.

Mr. HAMILTON. Mr. Congressman, thank you. That is essentially my point. Many of these countries are also our allies. There are geostrategic issues here having to do with common defense as well. And the message is important. So the message I suggest we consider is in fact to move ahead with a bilateral arrangement, as I said, but to embed it in a broader initiative across the North Atlantic with our close allies for jobs and growth. That would underpin the NATO alliance. That would give us all more opportunities. And we would be the global leader setting standards for the rest of the world.

Whether the other leg of this, is a TTIP-like thing or something else, that is probably not this discussion. But I would simply say the three points I outlined for a U.S.-U.K. arrangement that, besides tariffs, services, regulatory conformity, or a recognition, and new standards, pioneering new standards, is essentially the framework we could also use with the European Union.

Mr. KEATING. I would suggest, from my opinion, that it is precisely the time to be talking about this. The fact, whether you call it TTIP or some revision of that, this is the time to be talking about this, not moving ahead with one and leaving the other 80 percent of our allies by the wayside or giving that impression unintentionally. Because impressions are important in that regard.

Quickly I would like to just touch on a couple of other points. One is how can we make sure the U.S. companies currently in the U.K. continue to have access to the EU single market for our companies that are there? I would just like any suggestion about how we are going to navigate that.

And if you could, I will go to my third question because we are running out of time, if you could mention particularly the financial markets. How that could be the case?

Mr. HAMILTON. Yes, well, this is again important. The U.K.-EU dimension of this will determine how U.S. companies based in the U.K. will in fact access the single market. So those companies are reliant on the nature of that U.K.-EU deal. And with all due respect to the notion that they will do this quickly, EU and Canada have been negotiating an agreement for 7 years now. They have got it pretty far, but it is still not done. And that is just with Canada where there haven't been all those major types of issues. This is pulling the EU and the U.K. in a new way. I think it will just take longer.

So on financial services is exactly where all of this comes together because the U.K. banks, financial institutions, anything based in the U.K. will lose, as a matter of the Brexit, their automatic right called passporting rights to provide services throughout the rest of the European Union. They will lose that. Many U.S. banks and financial institutions rely on that passporting right to do their business in the rest of Europe, as I mentioned. There is now a U.K. equivalents regime, which is different, which says the EU says any non-EU jurisdiction that has equivalent procedures, say in financial services to the EU, they will accept some of those rights.

But it is a new regulation. It is inconsistent. It is uncertain whether it will continue for both the U.S. and the U.K. So this shows how we have to move in tandem with both tracks here and make sure that the U.K.-EU track also is in American interests. We should be actively engaged to square that triangle, if you will, with a view to our own interests. Because they are going to be massively effective.

Mr. KEATING. Thank you. And I will actually leave—I yield back a few seconds since we are a dual committee.

Mr. POE. I thank the gentleman.

The Chair recognizes the gentleman from California, Chairman Rohrabacher, for his questions.

Mr. ROHRABACHER. Well, thank you very much. I noted perhaps in a humorous way about the disruptive nature of our new administration. But let me just note that many of us on this side of the aisle, and especially yours truly, applauds the disruption of the way the system worked before. And clearly what we have here is an affirmation by the British people that the system needed to be disrupted for their wellbeing. They made that decision.

The EU and this getting into these large multilateral trade agreements was not to their benefit. That is why they voted not to stay in, what they—of course what appears to be, when people are negotiating, such bilateral agreements, what appears to be some sort of idealization of what could happen that is beneficial quite often results in what I think, the British people, found resulted in not a free trade but in controlled and regulated economic activity. Economic activity that was controlled and regulated by multinational bureaucrats set in Brussels. Or perhaps there is other places they have their offices as well.

Let us note that our President, Mr. Trump, has made himself very clear that all this talk about free trade. And I know our conservative and Republican think tanks have this image in their mind of what free trade means. I think free trade is something— I have always said I believe in free trade between free people. And if there is ever an example of two free people, it has to be Britain and the United States.

But in terms of how our free trade between us relates to the very other complications that you are talking about, they are the complications of what happens when you decide to organize your economic—international economic activity through a multilateral basis rather than a unilateral basis. And that is what President Trump is all about. He wants to shift away from the old system which gave too much power to people who are not involved with America's interests but perhaps a bureaucratic and systematic allegiance.

And just something you said, Mr. Hamilton, struck me. So the WTO is going to have to approve any agreement between England and the United States. Is that right? What is it? Where does the WTO come into this?

Mr. HAMILTON. The U.K. right now has a set of commitments by virtue of its membership in the European Union to the WTO. So if it leaves the European Union, it has to show the WTO its new commitments. So it is the WTO. It is nothing to do with any negotiation with us. But if we don't know what those commitments are, it is hard to start a negotiation. We don't know what the tariffs will be in the U.K. until they do that. They will have to do that first. And within the WTO, any member of the WTO could veto that until the U.K. does something that everyone will agree to. So I am just saying I think that it will get done. I don't want to make too much of it, but I think it will just prolong the timing. That was my main point.

Mr. ROHRABACHER. So what we have now is the greatest cheat and the greatest undermining of the wellbeing of American people, the Beijing regime, the clique that runs China, now has some sort of veto power of what kind of agreement we are going to have between Britain and the United States. They will determine whether or not it is consistent.

I remember when I first got here how several of us opposed the WTO entry in by China. We said, you know, again, free trade, free people. China is not in any way a free country. And much less in terms of their economics.

So let us just point out again that perhaps in the long term President Trump may have his finger on the right direction—pointed in the right direction. Let's start emphasizing good relations and economic activity on a bilateral basis with free people around the world like the Brits rather than putting our faith in multilateral organizational trade.

Thank you.

Mr. POE. The gentleman yields back his time.

And the Chair recognizes the ranking member, Mr. Meeks, from New York.

Mr. MEEKS. Thank you, Mr. Chairman.

Let me just make a quick comment. I am almost just the opposite of my chair. I think that the world is interconnected, and we are better interconnected, we are safer interconnected. When—one reason why that is, you just need to look at history, and if you look at World War II, for example, when everybody was looking at their own individual interest, it was war. They were fighting one another.

The reason why people came together, the interconnectedness, is to have more of a peacetime and to have a better future collectively. And so to say—and to have rules and order. The reason you have a WTO of multilateral organizations, so that you can set a rules-based society so that you don't have something where everyone is just going at it free willy-nilly, because then in this internet connected world, where would we be, where would we go?

So even when we are talking about Brexit and the possibility why I think that this—you know, I agree with Mr. Hamilton, you know, you can have some conversations understanding that it is, you know, something that is not going to happen for way down the road, you can be the cause of this happening. I think that if, in fact, there was negotiations on a free trade agreement, a bilateral free trade agreement with the U.K., that hurts the U.K. also. Because why would the EU—in the negotiation with the U.K. and the EU, they have got to negotiate, and if they see that Britain is trying to say, as I think, Mr. Gardiner, you can tell me if I heard you correctly, that you basically were advocating, because in your opening statement, everything you said about the EU was jump off this sinking ship, you know, it is bad, leave it alone, that you were somewhat advocating for the end of the EU as we know it, that it is out worn its relationship or its need of being, that USA, forget about the EU, just focus on United Kingdom. Is that correct?

Mr. GARDINER. If I could respond to that. And firstly, in my testimony, I made the point that Britain is far better off outside of the European Union. And I believe the Brexit is very good for the United States and for the British people because this is an issue of sovereignty and self-determination of freedom. You are not a sovereign nation if you are a member of the European Union. But I did not make a, you know, an assertion that——

Mr. MEEKS. Your exact quote, if I am not mistaken, is the declining EU.

Mr. GARDINER. Yes. It is a declining EU, that is correct. And if other nations within the EU wish to leave the European Union, that is their call.

Mr. MEEKS. Well, even Prime Minister May, in her statement, says we need a strong EU. It seems to me that even in the U.K.'s best interest, as stated by the Prime Minister herself, that she is advocating for a strong EU, that we need a strong EU, that in fact we don't need a declining EU, we have got to make sure that it is strong.

Mr. GARDINER. Well, that is up to European leaders to decide whether they are able to advance a strong European Union. There is no evidence at this time that the EU is becoming a stronger entity. It is certainly weakening, and the winds of change are blowing across Europe, and there is a drive toward sovereignty and self-determination that many EU elites simply do not accept.

Mr. MEEKS. Let me reclaim my time because I am running out. Mr.—Dr. Hamilton, let me just ask you a question. You mentioned that negotiations do not happen in a vacuum and that with the active negotiations with the WTO and Asia, the EU, that these all, these negotiations will be intertwined. So my first question would be—but all that seems like a lot to me. Does the U.K. even have the manpower? Because there is a lot of manpower, you got all of this negotiation, you got to do all this. Do they have—you know, I think the last time they negotiated a deal by themselves, I don't know when it was, to be quite honest with you.

So it seems to me—my first question is, you know, do they have the manpower to do this? Is it—you know, can you give me your thoughts on that?

Mr. HAMILTON. The government is quickly trying to get up to speed to get a bigger bench on trade, but as you correctly point out, they haven't been doing this for a long, long time since the EU has the authority to negotiate trade deals. So I was asked by the State Department some time ago to go brief a number of them coming over to try to figure out how to do all of this. But you are right, this is part of the issue.

The capacity, the sheer capacity of the U.K. to do all these things will be stressed. We should probably help them, to the extent we can. But my point again is we should be realistic about the timeline that will be in front of us, given all these things the U.K.

itself has to do, regardless of our piece of it. It will just take some time.

Mr. MEEKS. I am out of time.

Mr. POE. I thank the gentleman.

The Chair recognizes the gentleman from California, Colonel Cook, for his 5 minutes.

Mr. COOK. Thank you, Mr. Chair.

This very illuminating hearing, I was really getting involved in this, and then I heard the chair talk about limbo time, and I thought it was a flashback when I was in college at Fort Lauderdale, and maybe he was there at the same time, but I haven't heard that expression in quite awhile.

Anyway, some of the comments that you made there, a number of years ago, I was probably—had a much more favorable viewpoint of the EU, some of the things that happened in Greece, Italy, maybe the tremendous influence that Germany exercised. So you caught my attention, Dr. Hamilton, particularly about the World Trade Organization. And, you know, I respect a country; if the U.K. wants to leave the EU, I understand that.

The problem I am hearing is, I guess it is like anything in this world, because it is run by you guys, which are lawyers, is that you better know exactly what you are getting into, because it might not be that easy to get out of. And I want to know, is that an accurate—if you have advice for us, if we could influence this decision, at least I am hearing is, before we start—and by the way, I am all for more trade with the U.K. I think everything that has been mentioned about the past and everything like that.

But before we get into this, are there certain hidden things that if something goes south that—one comment, I think, Dr. Hamilton, you mentioned 8 years, and I know, Dr. Gardiner, you had a much shorter time in your argument about it.

But the point, I am trying to get your viewpoint, Dr. Hamilton, maybe you will give it, is that you better have your eyes wide open when you get into any trading arrangements. You know, I am a big NATO person, support the alliance and everything else, but you have to know exactly what you are getting into, and that is my takeaway. Can you comment on that briefly, anybody?

Mr. HAMILTON. You had referred to me. If I could, just briefly, you know, on the EU, much of this, these are our allies, almost all of them, and they have said this is the way they are trying to organize the peace in Europe, and as was mentioned, after World War II, after a world war, the survivors of war decided this is—by melding their economies, it is the way to prevent war. The United States provided, through NATO, an umbrella under which they could reconcile and create this type of effort.

American workers, consumers, companies all profit from that deep, deep relationship with the U.K. and also with the rest of our allies. So I think we should think about it in that, if I may.

You say keep your eyes open. Here are some issues. We say tariffs won't be a problem, but agriculture, that is likely to be a problem. British farmers are about to lose the subsidies that they get through the common agricultural policy through the EU, and then they will be in a trade agreement facing U.S. competition. That will be a domestic political issue in the U.K., I can guarantee it to you.

We have an issue with financial services on both sides of the Atlantic because the city of London believes that is their advantage.

We have resisted including financial services in the same kind of negotiation that we have had with the EU and TTIP because of other kinds of concerns. We will have to address the financial services issue in the way that I describe because it is so interlinked. So there are issues. I am not saying there aren't, even with the U.K., but if we don't go forward with this kind of agreement, then we will be looking at the WTO baseline, which is, as I mentioned, which means tariff barriers to U.S. products and services that otherwise we will—wouldn't have if we have an agreement.

Mr. COOK. Yeah. But my comment, you know, the takeaway from this is, obviously, the British people were unhappy with the situation. It is just like us. I understand the commitment to Europe, I understand the commitment to our allies and everything else, but it all comes back to our constituents. I don't represent anybody in the U.K. you know, I am worried about the issues in—and sometimes I think we all run the danger of getting out of touch with the people that we serve.

That is—you know, I love the Brits, I love the Europeans, I love everybody, kumbaya. But first and foremost, you know, the people of the 8th Congressional District, and that is, you know, why I raise my hand.

Some of the talk, as I said—and I am running out of time—is just to convey that fear that, you know, the World Trade Organization, and when certain things are happening in the economy and we get those cards and letters, we have to read them and respond to them.

I yield back.

Mr. POE. I thank the gentleman.

The Chair recognizes another gentleman from California, Mr. Sherman.

Mr. SHERMAN. Thank you.

We have had an election. The clear message is the American people are on the side of trade skeptics who don't think that the trade deals we have entered into in the past have been good. And what we are going to see is a bait-and-switch, because now we are being told that the only problem is multilateral trade deals.

Well, TTIP is a bilateral trade deal. Of course, we are a union of 50 States, they are a semi-union of dozens of states. NAFTA, which is held out to be the worst deal, you could call it a bilateral deal, but all the controversial provisions are the U.S.-Mexico provisions. If it was just a U.S.-Canada deal, I don't think it would be discussed much.

So NAFTA's controversial positions are, in effect, a bilateral deal. The South Korea deal, which cost us as much in jobs as any on a pound-for-pound basis, is a bilateral deal. So what we are going to be told is that the Wall Street elite should control American trade policy to the destruction of the American middle class, but we should insist that they do it on a case-by-case country-by-country basis.

I would submit that American workers should not compete with 40 cent an hour Vietnamese labor that cannot organize and has no freedom, whether it is part of a TPP or whether it is an individual deal.

Now, I have been told that our witnesses are generally trade-ophiles rather than trade skeptics. Is that a mischaracterization of any of you? No. And so, notwithstanding the wave and the message, the only loud message that came from the American people, those who support these trade deals continue to dominate the discussion here in Washington.

In looking at a trade deal, and there are some worthy of support, the issues that come up are investor-state, low wages, labor rights, environmental protection, currency manipulation, and balance of trade. Well, with Britain, low wages, I think, is one of the big problems because, in theory, a trade deal should equalize wages in both contracting parties. Well, British wages are relatively high. Labor rights, they have got stronger labor rights than we do.

Are any of our witnesses familiar with American right-to-work laws?

I don't see any, but I will point out that the State Department has testified before Judge Poe and my subcommittee back in the day that our right-to-work laws are a violation of the U.N. declaration of human rights and international labor standards because they, in effect, make it impossible to organize unions. Environmental protections are strong in Britain, viewed on a world standard, and I haven't seen serious currency manipulation.

So let's go back to investor-state. We are told, in other trade agreements, that we have to surrender our sovereignty and give giant corporations a second way to attack our environmental protections and consumer protections in order to give our corporations a fair shot when they are doing business abroad.

Do our witnesses generally agree that American business can get a fair shake in British courts, and therefore, it is not necessary to have investor-state protections for American corporations? Dr. Hamilton, if you can just give me a yes or no. I have to get through the list.

Mr. HAMILTON. Yes.

Mr. SHERMAN. Mr. Lester?

Mr. LESTER. Yes.

Mr. SHERMAN. Dr. Gardiner?

Mr. GARDINER. Yes.

Mr. SHERMAN. Balance of trade. Would a deal with Britain that simply eliminated all tariffs be good or bad for reducing America's trade deficit? Dr. Gardiner. Or it is possible that it can't be estimated, but if you have an estimate, let me know.

Mr. GARDINER. Well, it would be good for the trade deficit. It would be good for the U.S. economy.

Mr. SHERMAN. I didn't ask the economy.

Mr. GARDINER. Yeah.

Mr. SHERMAN. Would it—we have the largest trade deficit in the history of a million life. Would a trade deal with Britain make that worse or better or you don't know?

Mr. GARDINER. It would not make it worse. I think that the United States would benefit from such a deal.

Mr. SHERMAN. Okay. Mr. Lester?

Mr. LESTER. I can't estimate it, but I also don't think trade deficits are bad for the economy.

Mr. SHERMAN. We lose 10,000 jobs for every billion dollars of trade deficit. And if you are not one of those 10,000 people, then your statement—go on, Dr. Hamilton.

Mr. HAMILTON. U.S. has a trade deficit in goods with the European Union and the U.K., but it has a trade surplus in services.

Mr. SHERMAN. Yeah, and I am looking for the unified. Some trade skeptics only focus on goods and——

Mr. HAMILTON. And my point was——

Mr. SHERMAN [continuing]. The services matter as well.

Mr. HAMILTON [continuing]. If it can open up the services economy across the Atlantic, the United States stands to benefit considerably.

Mr. SHERMAN. Okay. And finally, I will point out that Britain has a health system that makes ObamaCare look like it came from the Cato Institute. And I yield back.

Mr. POE. The Chair recognizes the gentleman from South Carolina, Mr. Wilson.

Mr. WILSON. Thank you, Judge Poe and Chairman Rohrabacher, for calling this very important meeting and hearing. And thank you for being here today. It is very meaningful to me.

I was born into this special relationship with the U.K. I grew up in the most British city of North America, Charleston, South Carolina, and so we have always had such a great appreciation. And in my home State, the benefits of this have been immeasurable. Also, it is the birthplace of Congressman Greg Meeks, so I am sure he and I share the appreciation.

And it was really the British investment Bowater that was the first foreign investment in our State, which then led to Michelin of France and Bridgestone of Japan, Continental of Germany, Getty of Singapore. And now South Carolina is the leading manufacturer and exporter of tires to any State in the United States.

Additionally, we have foreign investments, working with Governor Carroll Campbell and the late Governor Jim Edwards, in BMW, and now soon Volvo and Mercedes Sprinter Benz. South Carolina is the leading exporter of cars of any State in the United States, and so trade is very important, and we love to see those X5s in London and anywhere else.

But that in mind, Dr. Gardiner, the new—a trade agreement, would this enhance the prospects of new jobs? What would be the prospects?

Mr. GARDINER. That is an excellent question, and I should point out that already 1 million U.S. jobs depend upon British investment here in the United States, and 1.25 million British jobs depend upon U.S. investment in the U.K. And I do believe a free trade agreement would be a job creator. It will advance prosperity on both sides of the Atlantic. There are similar wage levels in the U.K. and the U.S. It is not going to threaten American jobs.

And also, this is a—you know, this is a bilateral trade deal as opposed to TTIP, which is not a bilateral trade deal, as one of the members suggested earlier that it was a bilateral deal. TTIP simply is not. It is a multilateral deal, very, very different to a U.S.-U.K. free trade deal. And I believe that encouraging more British investment in the United States will create a considerable number of additional jobs here in the U.S., and that is good for the U.S. economy. It is good for American workers. The American worker has nothing to fear from a free trade deal with the United Kingdom, but really should embrace it.

Mr. WILSON. Thank you very much. And again, I am grateful. My home State of South Carolina has certainly benefited.

And, Dr. Hamilton, we have such an extraordinary bilateral security situation and friendship, partnership with the U.K. Would additional trade agreements enhance our security relationships?

Mr. HAMILTON. I believe they would. I believe, while not an economic NATO, as people have said, a balanced agreement both with the U.K. as a strong NATO ally and our other European allies would be a second anchor to our alliance. It would reassure our allies of our commitment to NATO because we would again be tying our economies together in ways that we had not yet done. It would reassure us that those allies will be outward looking and open to American goods, services, and ideas.

So it would be mutually reinforcing to the NATO alliance itself. If it creates jobs and greater prosperity on both sides of the Atlantic, it also allows us to afford the military expenses that we need to expend for NATO and help our European allies to step up their military contributions, which is what the Trump administration, I think Democratic administrations have all asked them to do.

If I could just say on the nature of a U.S.-U.K. deal. It is not the fact of the deal that is going to bring jobs. It is what is going to be in it. And I agree with all the points that have been made, but I return to this one point, which was so many American companies are based in the U.K. because of the access they have to the rest of Europe. And if this deal is done to the exclusion of that access, many American companies are going to rethink their presence in the U.K.

So we have to assure that as we move ahead on this bilateral track with the U.K., we also consider this other piece because it is actually so vital to all those jobs back here that we just discussed.

Mr. WILSON. And other jobs, Mr. Lester, are with financial services.

And with the Trump administration's efforts to eliminate or repeal Dodd-Frank, wouldn't this be beneficial to both of our countries to reduce regulations?

Mr. LESTER. Yes, it would. And in the TTIP, one of the hurdles was demands from Europe to loosen financial services regulation, make it easier for European financial services companies to operate in the U.S. And in this new context with the new administration, you know, sort of maybe rolling back Dodd-Frank a bit, that can only help our negotiations with both the rest of Europe and also U.K., in particular, should facilitate the trade deal. You know, we are sort of giving them what we want because we think it benefits us.

Mr. WILSON. Thank you very much.

Mr. POE. The gentleman yields back his time.

The Chair recognizes the gentleman from Rhode Island, Mr. Cicilline.

Mr. CICILLINE. Thank you, Mr. Chairman.

Dr. Gardiner, if I understand your testimony, both your testimony and your written testimony in which you say, "A free trade agreement would boost Britain and America's economies while also strengthen the Anglo-American special relationship, for decades the engine and beating heart of the free world." "A stronger Britain on the world stage, able to act as a truly sovereign, independent nation, is a far better partner for the United States."

That sounds to me like a very romantic view of times past and really disregards the current world context and is not even an economic argument but more of an idealogical or political argument. And the reason that I am questioning this is Prime Minister May said very clearly that it is in all of our best interest that the EU succeed. And she is very clear that that is critical to the future of the U.K. as well as the economic relationships.

She is the leader of the United Kingdom. Why is she wrong and you are right that a declining European Union and a relationship between the United States and the U.K. is better for the U.K. and the United States?

I mean, it seems that Dr. Hamilton's testimony about, thinking about this in a little more sophisticated way, of the U.S.-U.K., the U.K.-the EU and the U.S.-EU, particularly when these economies are all integrated and related and people's interest in markets are so dependent on each other's access to those markets, it seems like a kind of America first idea of just U.K. and U.S. over here, sort of disregarding the reality of these economic relationships. And why shouldn't we, as a matter of trade policy, be looking at engaging in these conversations simultaneously to maximize the benefits to American jobs, American workers, and the growth of the American economy?

What is the basis for your claim that we are better off just having Britain and the U.S. do a trade agreement? I mean, it doesn't seem like that—that doesn't make common sense to me, let alone be supported by any kind of economic analysis. I mean, is it simply, is it, sir, this yearning for those days of old?

Mr. GARDINER. Well, firstly, thank you very much for all your questions and to respond to them. First, this is not a romanticized view. The special relationship is a reality. It has been a reality for over 70 years. It is the engine of the free world. And when U.S. and British Forces fight together on the battlefield, as they have done on countless occasions defending the cause of freedom, that really does matter.

So I think that it is a tremendous reality. It is a very, very powerful force. And clearly, for the British people, they decided they were better off outside of the European Union. And with the—with the new British Brexit approach, Britain is going to be an even more outward looking nation that is going to work together with its allies and confront the enemies of freedom. And I think that, you know, this is not a romanticized view. This is the reality.

As for the future of the European Union—and Theresa May rightly pointed out that it is good to have a strong Europe for the United Kingdom, but, you know, the reality is within the European Union, there is deep-seeded discontent. You do have European leaders who seem to be deeply out of touch with a lot of their own electorates. European countries cannot control their own borders, and many of the rules that govern the European Union simply, you know, are unrealistic in this day and age with the rise of Islamist terrorism in Europe, the tremendous threats that we face across the world. And I think that, you know, Europe needs to adapt to the new realities. And the British people, their desire for freedom is shared by, you know, tens of millions of people across the EU as well.

Mr. CICILLINE. Thank you, Doctor.

Dr. Hamilton, could you speak to this? You know, I am not sure that the new administration takes the same view as Prime Minister May, the same view that all the Prime Ministers have taken about the importance of the success of the European Union.

Could you speak to what the benefits of that are as well as the dangers to the United States and the U.K. or to our interest if the EU fails and what we might do as Members of Congress to support the strength of the EU?

Mr. HAMILTON. Thank you. Well, as I said also about my question about trade, it is not the fact of the EU, per se, that is an American interest. It is what kind of EU, and how does it relate to the interest we actually do have.

You know, since the end of the Cold War and even before, Ronald Reagan, George Bush, every—both Bushes, and the Democratic Presidents have held the vision of a Europe whole and free. That has animated our policies toward Europe for a long time.

If we are facing or actively engaged in creating a Europe that is fractured and anxious, I would argue that is not an American interest and it will shortchange the American economy as well. It will mean a Europe that is beset by various nationalisms. That has not proven to be a good thing for America in our history. It is likely to be a Europe that is closed, in fact, then to American goods, services, and ideas, not one that is open. It is likely to be a Europe that at some point would come under the influence of a country or a group of countries hostile to the United States. We have experienced that in our history. Also not good for us. And if it is a fractured Europe, it is not going to be a partner. It is not going to be an ally. It is going to be a squabbling set of countries that will get us into trouble and draw blood and treasure away from all the other issues we have to deal with.

So if the EU can work toward the kind of Europe that I just identified, the opposite of all of that, we should support it. If it does things that don't do that, we should object. We should be—have a very clear-eyed view of our own interests regarding the European Union or NATO or our bilateral relationships. But at the moment, the kind of EU that is there is the one we need to deal with, and we need to see that we can work with it to steer it in this direction of a Europe that is whole, free, confident partner of the United States.

Mr. POE. The gentleman's time has expired.

Thank you, Dr. Hamilton.

The Chair recognizes the gentlelady from Nevada, Ms. Titus.

Ms. TITUS. Thank you, Mr. Chairman. It is a pleasure to be on this committee.

I have two questions. One is more politically oriented, and the other, policy. My political question is, is it not possible that those who are pushing this so-called special agreement between the U.S. and the U.K. now aren't just using this as a stalking horse to improve England's or the U.K.'s position in the Brexit negotiations?

And then my policy question has to do with you, Dr. Hamilton. You mentioned a lot about the service side of this, and I think that is very important, but most of the focus has been on financial services. I represent Las Vegas, so the tourist side of services is very important to our economy. If you look at the figures, just last year, over 5 million people came from the U.K. as tourists to the United States, 400,000 of those came to Las Vegas. They are our third largest visitor source after Canada and Mexico.

So I wonder if anybody is talking about the tourist aspects of any kind of special agreement and realizing that we can't wait 8 years for this to be looked at. And there is some very big issues. You look at the fact that the U.K. is part of the Visa Waiver Program. How does that continue? You look at policy toward refugees, policy toward immigrants, travelers, business travelers. I would just ask if anybody is investigating that or recognizing the importance of it, after you answer my political question.

Mr. GARDINER. If I could answer your first question, which is an excellent question about the Brexit negotiations with the European Union, how the U.S.-U.K., you know, free trade agreement impacts that.

I would point out firstly that Britain is already in trade discussions with a wide range of countries stretching from Australia, Canada, New Zealand, to India, and even South Korea with regard to free trade agreements. So of course, the United States free trade deal is the most important deal for the United Kingdom, but they are in discussions with many, many other countries. And I don't think that, you know, this is, you know, politically motivated, vis—vis, the Brexit negotiations with the European Union, which are an entirely different course.

And I think that, you know, if Britain was not in the European Union and had not been tied to the EU for the last four decades plus, Britain would already have signed a free trade agreement with the United States a very, very long time ago. And it is astonishing in this day and age that European countries are not able to negotiate their own free trade deals. There are countries that are part of the European Union, 28 countries, that do not have that freedom unless they leave the European Union. And that kind of centralized political power being asserted by Brussels is really a, you know, slap in the face for national sovereignty. And that was a big reason why the British people decided to exit the European Union, to exit—in order to implement that freedom to negotiate their own free trade agreements.

Ms. TITUS. Okay. Thank you.

Mr. HAMILTON. Madam, if I may, on your—the other part, on services. So there are, of course, a variety of services. Services are where all the jobs are across the Atlantic, and they are highly protected on both sides of the Atlantic. So instead of the goods tariffs, we should focus on services, including on people flows. And you are right, it is unclear exactly what the arrangements will be if the U.K. leaves the EU. We have to sort that out. I don't think it will be a problem, but I think we will need to sort it out.

But let me show you where we could move ahead. The digital economy. U.S. and Europe are the leaders in the digital economy. We are most linked with each other. And the U.S. And the U.K., in terms of e-commerce, are each other's most important partners in the world. Seventy percent of e-commerce buyers in the U.K. go to American sites to buy, and 49 percent of American consumers go to British sites to buy things. And yet the digital world is still in flux.

So it is about making sure we have high standards, we can set that pace because we are so deeply interlinked, and the digital economy is becoming the economy. So this would be, I think, very considerable.

Services are about qualifications. If an architect wants to work here or in the U.K., do we recognize those qualifications, legal qualifications? When I mention about mutual recognition, it might be to try to break down some barriers there that would facilitate the flow of highly professionalized services.

So these are the kinds of things that I think a U.S.-U.K. deal could actually set the pace on, but it needs to be done, as I keep saying, in some sort of balance with how we are going to work with the rest of our European allies.

Ms. TITUS. Never mind the tourism issue with the gaming issue, which is very important in Nevada, now you have got another complication.

Thank you, Mr. Chairman.

Mr. POE. The lady yields back her time.

The Chair recognizes Mr. Rooney from Florida for his questions. Perfect timing.

Mr. ROONEY. Thank you, Mr. Chairman.

Mr. POE. Microphone.

Mr. ROONEY. Yeah. Thank you, Mr. Chairman.

Mr. Lester, I would like to ask you a question. I would like to thank you for taking time to testify.

If a U.S.-U.K. trade agreement is going to be a gold standard, what are the building blocks we should look for that we can use to build future trade agreements on?

Mr. LESTER. This is a great question because one thing that we really need to talk about is what is the model of trade agreement that we are using? We spent the last decade with the same model, and it has worked well in some cases, you know, a few years ago, but lately we have been stuck. You know, we had the TPP and we had the TTIP following the same model, and we didn't get them done, and, you know, that is a problem.

And so the question is, if we do the same thing in the U.S.-U.K. trade agreement or any other bilateral trade agreement that we take on in the next couple of years, do they not get done? Do we spend the next 4 years negotiating something and then we don't have anything at the end of it? And that would be a huge problem if we go down that road.

So the question is what should be in this trade agreement? What are the building blocks?

And as much as people like to say tariffs are low, I would just like to point out some of them are high. There are these tariff peaks and tariffs are still a burden. They are taxes on trade, and we should do our best to get rid of as many as possible. So I think that is one of the—it has always been at the core of trade agreements and it should be at the core of trade agreements, get rid of as many tariffs as politically possible.

Beyond that, we talked a lot about regulations. Mr. Hamilton talked a lot about this already. And so there is this ambition out there in trade agreements that we are going to deal with all the regulatory trade barriers. And I am sympathetic and I would like to see it happen, but I think we should use caution and not try to overstate it.

We are probably not going to be able to have harmonized regulations between the U.S. and U.K., and I don't think we necessarily should. But there are more limited things we can do, and again, Mr. Hamilton has alluded to this. We can have mutual recognition. You know, sort of an accountant who is licensed to work in the U.S. Aren't they—you know, shouldn't they also be qualified to work in the U.K.? Can't we have some certification program to make that easier? So I think mutual recognition of certain products and services should be a core part of trade agreements.

So, now, beyond those tariffs and dealing with regulatory barriers, we have a lot of other issues that have traditionally been in trade agreements. Intellectual property and labor and the environment have been there for awhile. With the TPP, we brought in things like e-commerce and state-owned enterprises. All of this complicates the negotiation, and we just need to think carefully about what makes the most sense in the context of each specific negotiation.

So, you know, when we are talking about a U.S.-U.K. agreement, what should be in there, and, you know, how can that serve as a model for other agreements? You know, my personal preference is to focus on something like e-commerce. You know, a lot of our trade agreements, you know, haven't really adapted to the modern era of digital trade, so I think there is more we can do on e-commerce. But I do think we need to think carefully about what are all the elements that should be in there, what maybe could be excluded from the U.K. to get a trade agreement done more quickly and not go down the road of the TPP or TTIP where at the end of the day we don't have it.

Mr. ROONEY. Thank you.

I would also like to ask Dr. Gardiner a question here. I have got a little more time. Thank you for taking time to be here. As a banker and investor, I am especially concerned—and knowing London's preeminent position in the financial world, I am concerned about the asymmetries between the horrendous Dodd-Frank regulations and the free market capitalism of London, how, in this trade agreement process, can we resolve that, and do you have any advice for us what the Congress might do to reduce that asymmetry?

Mr. GARDINER. That is a very good—that is a very good question. And it should be pointed out the city of London is far bigger in terms of its financial clout than all of the other major European Union financial centers combined. And the city of London has prospered extremely well outside of the European single currency and I believe will continue to prosper outside of the European Union.

And you do raise, you know, an important question about asymmetry, and that is going to be, I think, a very, you know, significant issue in terms of the negotiations.

In my view, I believe that on both sides it is in the interest of the U.S. and British negotiators to ensure that U.S. investment can flow through the city of London and, similarly, for British investment to flow into New York and other U.S. financial centers. This is a tremendous creator of jobs and prosperity in the United States and also for the British people as well. There is a great deal at stake, and London and New York are the world's two largest financial centers, and no center in Europe can even compare to either of those. And it is in both sides interest to ensure that there are no barriers in place to doing—conducting deals between the two most important financial centers in the world.

Mr. ROONEY. Thank you. I yield back, sir.

Mr. POE. I thank the gentleman.

The Chair recognizes the gentleman from Pennsylvania, Mr. Boyle.

Mr. BOYLE. Thank you. And I thank the chairman and the ranking members of the subcommittees for holding this important hearing today.

I first wrote to Chairman Royce and Ranking Member Engel back in April, some 9 months ago requesting a hearing on what was then the possibility of Brexit. This is about 2 months before the—yeah, 2 months before the vote at that point, because I was concerned that many people in this town and on this side of the Atlantic were not taking the threat of a potential Brexit vote very seriously. And since late June, when that vote was made, I have been pushing for a hearing, because it will have great effect, not just on the U.K. and the EU, but also, of course, on the United States.

While I respect the right of the British voters to, of course, peacefully determine their own future as it relates to Europe and the rest of the world, and I look forward to maintaining the strong relationship that the U.S. and the U.K. currently enjoy, I do find Brexit deeply concerning for a number of reasons.

First, there is the question that some of my colleagues have mentioned on the future of the European Union itself. After centuries and centuries of warfare, the last 70 years that we have seen in Europe is the greatest time of peace and prosperity in the history of the continent. The European Union has played a incredibly important role in that integration, and anything that would threaten that is a threat not only to Europe, but frankly, the peace and prosperity that this country has enjoyed over that same period of time.

Second, Brexit does affect the U.K.'s overall influence within the EU. This is an issue, obviously, for the U.K., but it is also an issue for the United States. There are times in the 1980s, and especially when Tony Blair was prime minister, when the U.K.'s influence within the EU was able to benefit the U.S. and U.S. foreign policy interests. Will that now be jeopardized as the U.K. takes a step back from being a member of Europe?

Third, and the issue that hasn't been raised at all here today, I believe that it is a responsibility of the United States as one of the three guarantors of the Good Friday Agreement to make sure that there is nothing about Brexit that threatens the Good Friday Agreement.

The exit of the U.K. from the EU potentially threatens the commitment of the U.K. to human rights, brings in to question funding for peace-building initiatives in Northern Ireland, of which the European Union has been a major contributor, and the common travel area between Ireland and Northern Ireland. There simply cannot be any backsliding into the bad old days of border checkpoints.

So my question is to Mr. Hamilton. Given the outsized role that immigration and open borders had in fueling the Brexit vote and the potential tough line the EU will take in negotiations, how can the U.K. really negotiate a "no hard border" on that which is their only land border that exists between the EU and the U.K.?

Mr. HAMILTON. Thank you. Well, that is one more issue that will have to be resolved. It is unclear, I think, particularly to people in Ireland, about the impact of Brexit on their border and on this common travel space. Prime Minister May has said while it is a clean Brexit, as she said, they do want some sort of more porous arrangements between Northern Ireland and Ireland. How that will work is very unclear, given the British Government's attitude to really checking flows of people. So I think it is just one more detail that is unresolved.

Again, back to, as you said, we have a stake in some of this because of the role we played in bringing peace to that region, but we also have an economic stake. Ireland is also a major base for American companies exporting not only to Europe but to the rest of the world. American companies based in Ireland export more into world than, you know, companies in Mexico do. I mean, it is a major base. And if that is again unsettled, it is an interest that we have to look to.

So our interest is to make sure these things progress in some mutually reinforcing way that advance our own interests. That means we have to play an active role, not dictating to the other parties what should happen, but to make sure that our interests are made clear and we are seen as defending the rights of the American workers and consumers and companies. And the U.K.-Ireland relationship is one more unsettled issue that we have a very strong stake in.

Mr. POE. I thank the gentleman.

The Chair recognizes the gentleman from California, Mr. Issa. I wasn't going to put you in Colorado yet, but——

Mr. ISSA. Well, you know, last night I was honored to be with a gentleman from Colorado who is going to be our next Supreme Court justice, so I feel very Colorado right now. Of course, I am from the 9th Circuit, so I'm jealous of the 10th Circuit at times too. Dr. Gardiner, in the last round of questioning, things devolved into British or England versus Ireland, but I want to bring you back to the U.S. versus Great Britain as there are opportunities. One of the reasons that the transatlantic trade deal was never going to happen is they waited on agricultural issues till the end. Can you tell me, in your opinion, and Mr. Lester, you may be able to do too, how much better, easier, or more possible if Great Britain leaves—when Great Britain leaves the European Union, will it be for us to resolve some of the perennial issues of GMOs and other aspects that often make it impossible for U.S. agricultural products to have a fair opportunity to enter those markets?

Mr. GARDINER. Thank you for your question, Congressman. That is a great question to ask.

I would say, you know, firstly, that with regard to TTIP that you mentioned earlier, there were major problems in terms of U.S.-EU discussions because of the EU's common agricultural policy, which some in Britain would describe as a vast protectionist racket basically.

Mr. ISSA. That, we can agree on both sides of the aisle.

Mr. GARDINER. Yes. And you know, the common agricultural policy really is a disastrous policy, in my view. And once Britain leaves the European Union, it will not be subject to the common agricultural policy. That may impact some British farmers, but the common agricultural policy largely serves the interest of French farmers actually, rather than British farmers.

The agricultural sector in the United Kingdom is relatively small. About 80 percent of the U.K. economy is service oriented. Agriculture will be an issue, but I believe that the British Government will be advancing really, you know, the elimination of all tariff barriers. They will be looking not to have a system of subsidies in place for farmers as it currently is with regard to the European Union.

So I do believe there will be a lot of areas of common interest there. There will be, of course, frank detailed discussions on this that may be difficult at times, but I think the barriers involved in those discussions are far, far less significant than they are with regard to the TTIP.

Mr. ISSA. Well, in following up on that, and Mr. Lester may be able to weigh in too, there are always two agricultural issues. There is the agricultural principal products, meat, poultry, and so on, but there is also the enhanced technologies the United States leads the world in, in enhancing the yield for farmers.

How would you contrast where you think Great Britain would be on a willingness—and this is a democracy's question—a willingness to begin looking at technologies that enhance yield? Because one of the reasons for the disparity between Great Britain's production and the U.S. production is historic land. It is a smaller, rockier environment, but it is also the fact that the seed and other technologies are not accepted sometimes in the European continent that are used commonly here to increase yield.

Mr. LESTER. It is hard to say anything definitive about it because the U.K. hasn't had to make these decisions in a long time. It has all been outsourced to the European commission, to the EU institutions to do this. And so we are left with, you know, sort of looking at what U.K. consumers have said, consumer groups, what their farm groups say and try to speculate about it.

I agree with Dr. Gardiner. It would be better dealing with the U.K. than it has been dealing with the EU, but how much better? I mean, you know, to get into specifics, can we sell hormone-treated beef in the U.K.? You know, can we sell all these—as you point out, there is advanced technology products, GMOs. Can we sell those in the U.K.? Will we be able to?

I think there is a better chance. I would like to see this process go forward. I am hopeful. But I recognize that, you know, throughout Europe, there are—there are concerns that people express, some legitimate, some not, some just purely protectionist, and so I think there is no way to know until we try. Let's give it a shot. Let's make our best arguments for why these products are safe. Let's see what they say.

I do think we have to be careful. If it is the U.S. Government pushing this view on the U.K., there will be people there who react badly.

Mr. ISSA. Sure.

Mr. LESTER. So I think there is a way to do it where, you know, the companies come forward with evidence: Here is our products and here is why they are safe, and I think that can help.

Mr. ISSA. And that may be ultimately what we talk about in a process to get to those approvals. But let me close with one question.

Intellectual property. We have tried to harmonize intellectual property, including copyright and others, in the last agreement and around the world, and we failed. Quite frankly, in some cases, we are less progressive than Europe.

How do you see the smaller bilateral agreement giving us the ability to harmonize on patent, trademark, and copyright?

Mr. LESTER. Well, it is harder to harmonize because we do it on a bilateral basis, you are doing it, you know, one-on-one, and you might end up with 20 agreements that say slightly different things, depending on who you are negotiating with. So I think that is a definite harm, a definite problem with taking a bilateral approach. At the same time, maybe we have more leverage and so we can push a little bit harder on specific issues.

Mr. ISSA. Well, let me just give you an example. If terrestrial radio play in the United Kingdom, the Beatles or the Beach Boys or anybody gets a royalty. In the United States, they don't. In a harmonized world where we are trying to bring that together, is that, for example, something that could be on the table that would be much more difficult when you are looking at 22 nations or whatever number?

Mr. LESTER. That is right. First of all, everything is on the table, but, yes, if we have specific interests in common with the U.K. on these issues, we can use that as a model. We can put that—we can set a precedent in the U.S.-U.K. trade agreement to say, look, this is now binding international law. We have it in the text here. Now let's try to push it on to other countries to do. We can certainly take that approach with that issue or other similar ones.

Mr. ISSA. Excellent. Thank you, Mr. Chairman.

Mr. POE. The gentleman yields back.

The Chair recognizes the gentlelady from Florida, Ms. Frankel.

Ms. FRANKEL. Thank you, Mr. Poe. Thank you, gentlemen.

So let me just start by saying, I hope that Brexit was not just a extreme nationalistic reaction with unintended consequences of gigantic proportions because this is not just a simple divorce. The way I am looking at this, there is a lot of children and a lot of property out there, right?

So—and it sounds very complicated with a lot of moving parts, so but getting away from the politics, my first question is what do you see in terms of the new gateway? If Great Britain is divorcing itself from the European Union, and so much of our business has to do with the—what is the current situation, do you—what country, if any, or countries do you see as becoming the new gateway?

Mr. GARDINER. If I could respond to your question.

Ms. FRANKEL. Yes.

Mr. GARDINER. And I think that, you know, regardless of, you know, Brexit, U.S. investment will continue to flow into Great Britain. Great Britain will continue to be the gateway for U.S. companies operating in Europe. In fact, I would argue actually that, you know, with the strength of the British economy, Britain is the fastest growing economy in the G7, and the economic outlook actually for Brexit, Britain is extremely positive. That is good news for U.S. companies and investors.

And just as Britain thrived outside of the European single currency, many warned at that time that Britain would lose a lot of U.S. business, for example, by staying out of the euro, but quite the opposite happened, actually. And I think that you will see U.S. companies continuing to invest in a major way in the United Kingdom. After all, there is $5 trillion worth of U.S. corporate assets in the United Kingdom. That is 22 percent of all U.S. overseas corporate assets. I expect that to grow in the coming years.

Ms. FRANKEL. Do you gentlemen agree?

Mr. LESTER. I would—I mean, I agree in the sense that, yes, there will still be continued investment in the U.K. But if your question is, if U.S. companies want to participate in the single market, want to be part of the single market, where else in the EU might they invest in order to be able to do that? Just off the top of my head, I mean, Ireland is a prime candidate, and I know a lot of U.S. companies, you know, set up operations there.

You also look at maybe places like Germany, because it is so big, or the Netherlands, but I think it is a great question. It is not something I had thought about before. I don't know if—you know, a lot of what we are talking about today is kind of speculative so, you know, those are sort of my initial speculations.

Mr. HAMILTON. This relates back to the point that the terms between the U.K. and the EU will affect U.S. corporate decisions. So the U.K. is the gateway to the rest of Europe for many companies. American companies and our trade negotiators will want to know how open is that gateway, how wide is it, how strong is it going forward before they want to make their own investment decisions? I agree there will continue to be U.S. flows, but again, this is not an exclusive thing.

U.S. investment in the Netherlands is greater than in Britain. Ireland, as I mention, is another—the next biggest investment location. If the gateway is cracked and if it is not so open and it is not very wide, then they will make other decisions. There are already many alternatives. On the financial services, I think you will look to other centers like Frankfurt, which is the heart of the eurozone to benefit from U.S. corporate decisions.

So it is very speculative, as was said. But again, I come back to the basic point. We cannot look at this in some exclusive bilateral way. There are many other factors that will affect the position and the future of U.S. corporate presence in Europe and in the U.K.

Ms. FRANKEL. So let me—I see we only have 37 seconds, so maybe you can—I think I am the only one left, right?

Mr. POE. Yes, you are.

Ms. FRANKEL. I am between them and lunch here.

One of the—so just following from that, Dr. Hamilton, what are some practical consequences for American businesses as we wait for a decision? What is some action?

Mr. HAMILTON. Business usually doesn't like uncertainty or volatility. So I agree, if we can have some discussions bilaterally with the U.K., I think that helps. I think if we can have other discussions with the EU colleagues, that helps. And we need to understand the state of the U.K.-EU discussions to be able to provide some sort of sense of orientation.

My point is this will go on for a number of years. It is not something we can resolve easily now. And we should understand that, as you said, Brexit has set forth now a whole series of interconnected pieces of a puzzle, and we should be very clear about U.S. interests on all of those pieces going forward and that each piece of that stool, as I said, the transatlantic stool have to be strong and sturdy. That is the fundamental U.S. interest going forward, to convey some reassurance, not only to our allies, but also to our own companies and workers.

Ms. FRANKEL. Thank you.

I yield back. Thank you, Mr. Chair

Mr. POE. I thank the lady from Florida.

Without objection, a letter from the Software and Information Industry Association supporting the bilateral agreement between the U.K. and the U.S. will be admitted into the record for all purposes.

I want to thank all the witnesses for being here. I think it has been a very informative discussion. I am just glad I am not involved in trying to make an agreement between anybody now, but thank you for your expertise. And this subcommittee is adjourned.

[Whereupon, at 11:58 p.m., the subcommittees were adjourned.]

APPENDIX

MATERIAL SUBMITTED FOR THE RECORD

JOINT SUBCOMMITTEE HEARING NOTICE
COMMITTEE ON FOREIGN AFFAIRS
U.S. HOUSE OF REPRESENTATIVES
WASHINGTON, DC 20515-6128

Subcommittee on Terrorism, Nonproliferation, and Trade
Ted Poe (R-TX), Chairman

Subcommittee on Europe, Eurasia, and Emerging Threats
Dana Rohrabacher (R-CA), Chairman

TO: MEMBERS OF THE COMMITTEE ON FOREIGN AFFAIRS

You are respectfully requested to attend an OPEN hearing of the Committee on Foreign Affairs, to be held jointly by the Subcommittee on Terrorism, Nonproliferation, and Trade and the Subcommittee on Europe, Eurasia, and Emerging Threats in Room 2172 of the Rayburn House Office Building (and available live on the Committee website at http://www.ForeignAffairs.house.gov):

DATE: Wednesday, February 1, 2017

TIME: 10:00 a.m.

SUBJECT: Next Steps in the "Special Relationship" – Impact of a U.S.-U.K. Free Trade Agreement

WITNESSES: Nile Gardiner, Ph.D.
Director
Margaret Thatcher Center for Freedom
The Heritage Foundation

Mr. Simon Lester
Trade Policy Analyst
Herbert A. Stiefel Center for Trade Policy Studies
Cato Institute

Daniel S. Hamilton, Ph.D.
Executive Director
Center for Transatlantic Relations
Johns Hopkins School of Advanced and International Studies

By Direction of the Chairman

The Committee on Foreign Affairs seeks to make its facilities accessible to persons with disabilities. If you are in need of special accommodations, please call 202/225-5021 at least four business days in advance of the event, whenever practicable. Questions with regard to special accommodations in general (including availability of Committee materials in alternative formats and assistive listening devices) may be directed to the Committee.

COMMITTEE ON FOREIGN AFFAIRS

MINUTES OF SUBCOMMITTEE ON _Terrorism, Nonproliferation, & Trade and Europe, Eurasia, & Emerging Threats_ HEARING

Day _Wednesday_ Date _February 1, 2017_ Room _____2172_____

Starting Time _10:05 a.m._ Ending Time _11:58 a.m._

Recesses ☐ (____to____) (____to____) (____to____) (____to____) (____to____) (____to____)

Presiding Member(s)

Chairman Ted Poe

Check all of the following that apply:

Open Session ☑   Electronically Recorded (taped) ☑
Executive (closed) Session ☐   Stenographic Record ☑
Televised ☑

TITLE OF HEARING:

Next Steps in the "Special Relationship'"– Impact of a U.S.-U.K. Free Trade Agreement

---

SUBCOMMITTEE MEMBERS PRESENT:

Reps. Poe, Keating, Rohrabacher, Meeks, Wilson, Sherman, Issa, Sires, Marino, Cicilline, Cook, Frankel, Zeldin, Kelly, Sensenbrenner, Boyle, Rooney, Titus, Fitzpatrick, Torres, Schneider

NON-SUBCOMMITTEE MEMBERS PRESENT: _(Mark with an * if they are not members of full committee.)_

HEARING WITNESSES: Same as meeting notice attached? Yes ☑ No ☐
(If "no", please list below and include title, agency, department, or organization.)

STATEMENTS FOR THE RECORD: _(List any statements submitted for the record.)_

SFR submitted by Reps. Poe, Marino, and Sensenbrenner on behalf of the Software & Information Industry Association

SFR submitted by Rep. Marino

TIME SCHEDULED TO RECONVENE _____
or
TIME ADJOURNED _11:58 a.m._

Subcommittee Staff Director

MATERIAL SUBMITTED FOR THE RECORD BY THE HONORABLE TED POE, A REPRESENTA-
TIVE IN CONGRESS FROM THE STATE OF TEXAS, AND CHAIRMAN, SUBCOMMITTEE ON
TERRORISM, NONPROLIFERATION, AND TRADE, THE HONORABLE TOM MARINO, A
REPRESENTATIVE IN CONGRESS FROM THE COMMONWEALTH OF PENNSYLVANIA, AND
THE HONORABLE F. JAMES SENSENBRENNER, JR., A REPRESENTATIVE IN CONGRESS
FROM THE STATE OF WISCONSIN

SIIA Accelerating Innovation in
Technology, Data & Media

202.289.7442   1090 Vermont Ave NW Sixth Floor
www.siia.net   Washington DC 20005-4905

January 31, 2017

The Honorable Ted Poe
Chairman, Foreign Affairs Sbcmte. on
Terrorism, Nonproliferation and Trade
U.S. House of Representatives
Washington, D.C. 20515

The Honorable Dana Rohrabacher
Chairman, Foreign Affairs Sbcmte. on
Europe, Eurasia, and Emerging Threats
U.S. House of Representatives
Washington, D.C. 20515

The Honorable William Keating
Ranking Member, Foreign Affairs Sbcmte. on
Terrorism, Nonproliferation and Trade
U.S. House of Representatives
Washington, DC 20515

The Honorable Gregory Meeks
Ranking Member, Foreign Affairs Sbcmte.
on Europe, Eurasia, and Emerging Threats
U.S. House of Representatives
Washington, DC 20515

Dear Chairmen Poe and Rohrabacher, and Ranking Members Keating and Meeks,

On behalf of the Software & Information Industry Association (SIIA), thank you for holding the
upcoming joint hearing, "Next Steps in the "Special Relationship"–Impact of a U.S.-U.K. Free Trade
Agreement." SIIA shares your enthusiasm about opportunities for the United States to negotiate a
trade agreement with Great Britain, one of our most critical, long-standing trading partners.

SIIA is the principal trade association for the software and digital information industries. The more
than 700 software companies, data and analytics firms, information service companies, and digital
publishers that make up our membership serve nearly every segment of society, including business,
education, government, healthcare and consumers. As leaders in the global market for software
and information products and services, they are drivers of innovation and economic strength—
software alone contributes $425 billion to the U.S. economy and directly employs 2.5 million
workers and supports millions of other jobs.

An agreement between our two countries provides an opportunity to promote strong, sustainable,
balanced, and inclusive growth – which directly benefits U.S. companies and workers. As the Trump
administration directs focus away from multilateral trade agreements, towards a bilateral approach
to trade, U.S.-U.K. negotiations can provide the foundation of this approach, providing for the free
flow of information, ideas, and knowledge between these two strong economies. To foster
technological innovation and maximize job growth here in the United States, key elements of such
an agreement must include a provision prohibiting the mandated disclosure of software source code
or discrimination based on country of origin, and provisions allowing cross-border data flows and
permitting the use of data analytics while prohibiting mandated data localization. Exceptions to the
measures allowing cross-border data flows and prohibiting data localization should be permitted
only when necessary for the purpose of enforcing legitimate public policy measures, and must be
non-discriminatory and impose the least possible restrictions on data flows.

Software & Information Industry Association

Again, thank you for your leadership on this important issue. SIIA is strongly supportive of the opportunity to establish a bilateral Free Trade Agreement between the U.S. and U.K., and we look forward to working with Congress and the Trump Administration to achieve a deal that is to the benefit of not only the U.S. technology industry, but also American workers and consumers.

Sincerely,

Ken Wasch
President

cc: Members of the Subcommittee on Terrorism, Nonproliferation and Trade
    Members of the Subcommittee on Europe, Eurasia, and Emerging Threats

Congressman Tom Marino
TNT/EE&ET Joint Subcommittee Hearing
Next Steps in the "Special Relationship"–Impact of a U.S.-U.K. Free Trade
Agreement
Statement for the Record

Our alliance with the United Kingdom is one that has been enduring and consistent over time.

In voting to leave the European Union, the citizens of the UK decided that they wanted to have a greater say in how their country is managed. I applaud their decision, and wish them the best moving forward, and encourage the continuation of our special relationship.

An obvious first step is in further strengthening ties between the UK and the US through a new bilateral trade agreement.

Much uncertainty surrounds the timing of a trade agreement but both the US and the UK have signaled strong intentions to begin working towards one.

We have already seen UK Foreign Secretary Boris Johnson and Prime Minister Theresa May meet with the Trump Administration to begin these preliminary talks.

A possible trade agreement between the UK and the US would present an important opportunity to establish an international model for trade in creative goods and services.

As a member of the Judiciary Committee's Subcommittee on Courts, Intellectual Property and the Internet, I have seen the importance of protections for intellectual property.

Intellectual property in the US and the UK supports millions of high-paying jobs. All manner of content creators- from movies, music and books to software, apps and video games support more than 5.5 million jobs in the US and contributes $1.2 trillion dollars to US GDP. This totals nearly 7 percent of the US economy.

It's a similar situation for the UK, where the creative industries added £84.1bn in 2014 to their economy which accounts for over 5 percent of the UK economy.

Both the US and the UK are major exporters of creative goods and services because we both value freedom of speech and property rights.

I am hopeful that our countries can craft an agreement that will further facilitate trade and investment between our two nations by opening markets and providing robust protections for intellectual property.

While there are still many aspects of Brexit to resolve moving forward I hope that we can begin working towards an agreement that not only works for both countries and makes both countries stronger.